A Word That Sets Free

First Lesson Sermons For Sundays After Pentecost (Last Third) Cycle C

Mark Ellingsen

CSS Publishing Company, Inc., Lima, Ohio

A WORD THAT SETS FREE

Copyright © 2000 by
CSS Publishing Company, Inc.
Lima, Ohio

All rights reserved. No part of this publication may be reproduced in any manner whatsoever without the prior permission of the publisher, except in the case of brief quotations embodied in critical articles and reviews. Inquiries should be addressed to: Permissions, CSS Publishing Company, Inc., P.O. Box 4503, Lima, Ohio 45802-4503.

Scripture quotations are from the *New Revised Standard Version of the Bible*, copyright 1989 by the Division of Christian Education of the National Council of the Churches of Christ in the USA. Used by permission.

Library of Congress Cataloging-in-Publication Data

Ellingsen, Mark, 1949-
  A word that sets free : first lesson sermons for Sundays after Pentecost (last third) Cycle C./Mark Ellingsen.
    p. cm.
  Includes bibliographical references.
  ISBN 0-7880-1725-X-2 (alk. paper)
    1. Pentecost season—Sermons. 2. Bible. O.T.—Sermons. 3. Sermons, American. 4. Lectionary preaching. I. Title.
BV4300.5 .E55 2000
252'.64—dc21   00-035807
                                                                                                          CIP

This book is available in the following formats, listed by ISBN:
  0-7880-1725-X Book
  0-7880-1726-8 Disk
  0-7880-1727-6 Sermon Prep

For more information about CSS Publishing Company resources, visit our website at www.csspub.com.

PRINTED IN U.S.A.

*To Betsey
My favorite companion
in liberating adventures*

Table Of Contents

Introduction 7

Proper 21 11
Pentecost 19
Ordinary Time 26
    Even Our Business Belongs To God!
    Jeremiah 32:1-3a, 6-15

Proper 22 19
Pentecost 20
Ordinary Time 27
    When Life Gets Hard, Christian, Rebel!
    Lamentations 1:1-6

Proper 23 27
Pentecost 21
Ordinary Time 28
    In, But Not Of The World: A Spiritually
      Enriching, Liberating Experience
    Jeremiah 29:1, 4-7

Proper 24 35
Pentecost 22
Ordinary Time 29
    Your Sins Are Remembered No More; You're Free!
    Jeremiah 31:27-34

Proper 25 43
Pentecost 23
Ordinary Time 30
    A Fresh Start!
    Joel 2:23-32

Proper 26   51
Pentecost 24
Ordinary Time 31
    Life's Not Always Fair: But God Will Straighten It Out!
    Habakkuk 1:1-4; 2:1-4

Proper 27   59
Pentecost 25
Ordinary Time 32
    Living Free
    Haggai 1:15b—2:9

Proper 28   65
Pentecost 26
Ordinary Time 33
    A Vision Of Freedom
    Isaiah 65:17-25

Christ The King Sunday   73
    Salvation Includes Social Justice
    Jeremiah 23:1-6

All Saints' Sunday   81
    Why Earthly Powers No Longer Enslave
    Daniel 7:1-3, 15-18

Thanksgiving Day   89
    God's Gifts Are Free: Enjoy!
    Deuteronomy 26:1-11

Lectionary Preaching After Pentecost   95

Introduction

The sermons in the book are for a time of the year when congregational life is moving into high gear. The summer slump has ended, and the congregational programs have been renewed as autumn begins. (Regardless of what the liturgical calendar and the lunar calendar tell us, the new year in parish life begins in the fall.)

This is a time in the life of the Church for new programs, creative visions, and innovative ideas. Parishioners may be ready to hear fresh thinking and be challenged from the pulpit. But why would we look to Old Testament texts to inspire new, liberation insights and look to these texts for a freeing Word? After all, it is to the gospel of Jesus Christ in the New Testament that Christians look to find the liberating Word which sets free and creates the new situation (John 8:31-36; Galatians 3:10-14; 5). The Old Testament is about the Law and the confining demands of tradition. It is in the New Testament that the gospel and its freeing Word is to be found.

Such attitudes permeate the thinking of many Christians. It is one of the reasons that only a few of us typically look to the Old Testament for sermons. The history of Christianity indicates what a mistake this is. Martin Luther, the champion of Christian freedom, was primarily a scholar of the Old Testament, delivering most of his university lectures on that subject.[1] The Black church in America has likewise based its traditions of liberation in the Old Testament stories and prophetic traditions.[2] Perhaps one of the reasons that much American Christianity has been an advocate of the status quo and not very inclined to address socio-political issues relates to its failure to learn these lessons of the past. Such insights have not come easily for me. I have discovered them on my adventures in the gospel.

Christian life and Christian ministry are wonderfully freeing experiences. They set you free from old, often destructive habits and outlooks. Life really has been an adventure ever since I first truly understood the Gospel's freeing Word and affirmation of who I am. I have traveled to serve in positions and cultures as diverse as Pennsyvania Dutch rural ministry, to denominational seminary teaching in the Midwest, to international ecumenical work in Strasbourg, France, and to a faculty position in the largest predominantly Black seminary in the world. Along the way I have been engaged in many intellectual-spiritual adventures, several times changing my theological perspective, as circumstances and further study taught me the inadequacies of the old "truths" of which I was once so certain. Thus it was my professors at Yale University and the experience of preaching to my parishes in Pennsylvania that taught me to appreciate Luther's positive assessment of the Old Testament and the value of these texts for ministry. More recently it has been my immersion in the African-American church and in Black Theology that has helped me recognize how the Old Testament Word is a powerful witness for social change.

Many of the sermons in this book attempt to put to use what I have learned in this connection from the African-American Christian community that this son of Norwegian immigrants is now privileged to serve. Lately I have been trying to combine these insights of the Black church and its story-telling traditions with the appreciation of the Bible's narrative character and the spirit of adventure that my Norwegian immigrant elders and professors at Yale taught me earlier.[3]

What's next? Those set free by the gospel cannot answer that question definitively by providing a fixed plan for their lives. That would be a life of bondage. These sermons try to convey to hearers that the certainty that we have in our journeys is that God travels along with us and affirms us in our efforts, ever forgiving the dumb mistakes we make both individually and collectively. They also endeavor to remind us that our freedom is abused unless the gospel's freedom launches us into adventures aiming to liberate everyone else. In such adventures I have one other (penultimate) certainty, a wonderful companion who travels with me. And so this book is dedicated to my best friend and wife of 27 years whose company makes all the adventures I have in life even more fun.

---

1. For this assessment, scholars are indebted to the insights of Heinrich Bornkamm, *Luther und Das Alte Testament* (Tübingen: J. C. B. Mohr, 1948), p. 6.

2. For a similar assessment, see C. Eric Lincoln and Lawrence H. Mamiya, *The Black Church in the African American Experience* (Durham and London: Duke University Press, 1990), p. 202.

3. The narrative style of many of the sermons in this volume is expression of my own reliance on the methods of Post-liberal Biblical Narrative Theology. For insights into these methodological suppositions, see my *The Integrity of Biblical Narrative: Story and Theology in Proclamation* (Minneapolis: Fortress Press, 1990).

Proper 21 • *Pentecost 19* • *Ordinary Time 26*

Even Our Business Belongs To God!

Jeremiah 32:1-3a, 6-15

The weekend is shot (almost). Tomorrow it is back to the "real" world, back to the grind, at least for most of us. Where will God be in all that?

Be honest with me: Do you feel God's Presence on the job, as you go through the usual Monday routine? Is God directing you as you attend to your e-mail, run through your voice mail, review the reports, or check your assignment? Let us be frank with each other. The businesses which employ most of us are part of the "secular" realm, not of the "sacred" realm that concerns God. That is the way most Americans see it. Religion is one thing; business is another. Our commitment to the principle of separating church and state has led to a "culture of disbelief," one in which it is all right to be religious in private, but not publicly when we are on the job.[1] But that is not the way that the Bible views the world of business! This morning's First Lesson makes that clear.

Our text, Jeremiah 32, is the most detailed account of a business transaction recorded in the Bible. It is all about Jeremiah's purchase of land in Anathoth (a town just three miles north of Jerusalem) from his cousin Hanamel. What follows are all the details of the purchase regarding the cost, the signing of the deed, and the witnesses. What are details like that doing in the Bible, and what do they have to do with us?

It was a tense, really almost hopeless time. The Southern Kingdom of Judah (ruled by David's heirs and possessing the great capital of Jerusalem and its Temple) had been in decline for some time. The Babylonian Empire had set its sights on the Kingdom. In fact

Jerusalem was under attack (Jeremiah 32:2). Life as the Hebrews had known it, was not the same. They felt themselves to be witnessing the decline of their civilization, almost the end of the world. And we sometimes lament about the state of American society — its moral compass, declining standards, and selfishness. We "ain't seen nothing" compared to what the Hebrews in Jeremiah's day were experiencing.

It was hardly a time to trust the market or to make investments. Judah was a sinking ship. Our Bible lesson tells us that Jeremiah himself was in even more dire circumstances. He had been imprisoned by Judah's King Zedekiah for prophesying (correctly) that Jerusalem would be conquered by the Babylonians, that Judah's alliance with Egypt would not do it any good (Jeremiah 32:1, 3a; 37-38). And yet the Lord God came to the Prophet and told him to redeem land that was owned by his extended family, to buy that land (Jeremiah 32:6). (In ancient Hebrew culture when your extended family incurred debts and needed to sell land, the first right of purchase was given to next-of-kin to hold the property on the kin's behalf [Leviticus 25:25-28].) It was not smart business. But it seems that God has his own business strategies. He is going to turn a profit, even if it defies our economic theories. All our Bible lessons for today make that point. What we think is *our* business, ultimately *belongs to God.*

No, it did not seem to be a very good investment for Jeremiah to buy that land, what with the Babylonian conquest of the region on the horizon. The point that God seemed to want to make was that although appearances and ordinary perceptions appeared to render it a bad deal, in the divine plan, in the long run, it would work out for good. It was a good deal for Jeremiah to hold that land for his relatives, because someday the Hebrews would hold their land again in peace, even if in the short term the Babylonians would conquer. History has shown that Jeremiah and God were correct. The Hebrews did return from Babylon and the land surrounding Jerusalem (in Jeremiah's hometown of Anathoth) became their own again. After centuries of exile, that land is again in the hands of the Jews. When God gets into our business, he eventually produces results.

We get more of those unusual divine business strategies in our other assigned Bible lessons. In our Second Lesson from 1 Timothy 6 we hear that "the love of money is a root of all kinds of evil" (v. 10) and that those who are rich are not to be haughty or set their hopes on their riches, but are to be generous (vv. 17-18). The Gospel Lesson from Luke 16:19-31 echoes these themes with the story of the Rich Man and Lazarus. The rich man ignored the needs of the poor man Lazarus, and we learn that that was not God's way. His way is that you do not get hung up on wealth, and that if you have it, you use it generously for the sake of the poor.

These are nice ideals, but they will not work on the job tomorrow, will they? The boss expects you to make money for the company. The entrepreneurs among us know that you have to keep expanding the company, you have to increase its wealth, in order to "grow" the business. This brings us back to the concerns I raised at the beginning of this sermon. Where will God be when you get back to work tomorrow? Are the teachings of Jesus and the ideals of the Bible really applicable to the everyday business world, to the work-a-day world? At first glance they do not seem to be, and so on Monday we push our Christianity aside. Maybe that is why work is so unfulfilling for so many people. God does not seem to be present, and so work seems pointless, just a way to make a living.

This is precisely the point of our assigned Bible lessons and of this sermon. At first glance, it seems that God's ways cannot be related to what we do on the job. But it is God's style to surprise us with his ways. That is precisely what he did on the Cross. What to the world appeared to be the end of Jesus and his apparently insignificant and failed mission became God's way of giving life to all.

The sixteenth-century reformer, Martin Luther, called this manner of God's behavior the Theology of the Cross. God's style of working on the Cross, Luther claimed, continues to the present time. Just as God confronted the world and its wisdom on the Cross, so today we must learn to distrust our own wisdom and not rely on our own insight.[2] Why? Because "the works of God are always unattractive and appear evil...."[3] God works in this hidden way to humble us by confounding our wisdom. Then we will see how foolish and sinful we are and become totally dependent on him (1 Corinthians 1:20-29). Commenting on Psalm 30, Luther claimed:

> *We must not judge by what we feel or by what we see before us. The Word must be followed, and we must firmly hold that these truths are to be believed, not experienced; for to believe is not to experience. Not indeed that what we believe is never to be experienced but that faith is to precede experience. And the Word must be believed even when we feel and experience what differs from the Word.*[4]

Luther has helped us to understand why the Bible's business strategies seem so much in tension with our usual everyday business sensibilities. It has to do with God's style of confounding our worldly wisdom in order to make us recognize our total dependence on him.

But again we must consider how all this can be of any use to your tomorrow on the job. Recall Luther's comments that the Word of God will be experienced sometimes. It connects with our daily lives. That is the point of our First Lesson when it accounts in full detail the exact nature of the business transaction in which Jeremiah engaged. To paraphrase Luther: Your faith can connect with your daily business dealings, with your everyday life. But faith in that Word must precede your everyday experience. Interpret your job and its responsibilities in light of the Word of God.

What happens when you do that? What happens when you see your job in light of the Good News of God's forgiving love for you and me? That's when you truly can begin to feel that your business is really God's business.

Let's consider first the state of business in America. How do you feel about your job? Social analysts tell us that there is a great deal of anxiety out there about our jobs. The new economy values flexibility and openness to risk. But those dynamics create personal anxiety and apprehension. They also undermine a sense of mutuality, trust, and community. My primary agenda needs to be openness to new opportunities that can open doors for me, not to what is best for the company or my colleagues.[5] In these circumstances it becomes natural to feel that what you do on the job does not have much lasting spiritual significance. Is that the way work feels for you?

I hope it is not that way for you. Unfortunately, that futility is the way work feels for many of us. But even if you love your job, do you really see it as a ministry, like mine, one with lasting spiritual significance? I hope you do, but in case you do not, this sermon is for you.

Our First Lesson from Jeremiah about the Prophet's business transaction witnesses to the spiritual significance of business, of *your* job. By buying that land Jeremiah became God's vehicle for proclaiming that the Hebrew people would maintain the land of Judah, at least be returned to the land God promised (Jeremiah 32:26-44). Of course that was not obvious; God's ways are never obvious to common sense. (That is the essence of the Theology of the Cross.) Even Jeremiah had his doubts (Jeremiah 32:24-25).

Another Old Testament book praises the virtues of work, even though it does not seem very virtuous. The book of Ecclesiastes, probably composed at another time in Jewish history when the Hebrew people were enduring foreign domination, laments about the meaninglessness of life (1:1-11; 2:12ff.). Yet in the midst of this sense of chaos and meaninglessness, the sort of meaninglessness you may feel sometimes with your work, the Preacher who authored Ecclesiastes writes: "There is nothing better for mortals than to eat and drink, and find enjoyment in their toil. This also, I saw, is from the hand of God; for apart from him who can eat or who can have enjoyment?" (2:24-25). Work is one of the good things in life. Of course it is only enjoyable because it belongs to God, is one of God's good gifts.

Do you see your job that way, as a gift from God? The book of Ecclesiastes urges you to see it that way. "Not my job," you say. "It's a rat-race; it's dog-eat-dog. God can't be in that." Don't forget how God works in surprising ways, often confounding what we take to be common sense (the Theology of the Cross).

Work, your job, is a wonderful gift of God (even if it does not always seem to be). Believe it! As Martin Luther has put it:

> *Your work is a very sacred matter. God delights in it, and through it he wants to bestow his blessing on you. This praise of work should be inscribed on all tools, on the forehead and the face that sweat from toiling. For the world does not consider labor a blessing. Therefore it flees and hates it ... But the pious, who fear the Lord, labor with a ready and cheerful heart; for they know God's Command and Will.*[6]

Our work, Luther says, is a mask that God uses to give us his blessing. If we have earned any wealth by our work, if you are "comfortable," it is not you who earned it. Not really. God gave us these successes and the ability to achieve them as unmerited gifts.[7]

Do you get the implications of this for the importance of your work? If God uses your work as a "mask" for giving you the goods of life, then God uses your work and the work of others to give other people the necessities of life too. Sometimes, quite often, you can be God's means of working good for others. As much as my work brings God's love to people, your job provides these opportunities too. Your job is a spiritual vocation filled with ultimate meaning!

This is how the references in our other assigned Bible lessons to not flaunting wealth and to generosity to the poor become pertinent (1 Timothy 6:17-18; Luke 16:19-31). See your job as an opportunity to share God's love with your fellow human being. The greatest Reformed theologian of the past century, Karl Barth, put it this way: "Fundamentally, we can work aright only when we work hand in hand. The nourishing bread to be gained from work can only be bread broken and shared with the fellow-worker."[8] Work is not meant solely for profit, but for the service of the whole human community, so says the *Catechism of the Catholic Church*.[9]

Of course this idea that work should be for the sake of the community seems to go against the grain of the new dynamics of our economy, which, as we have noted, demand risk and flexibility, not loyalty and concern about community. But recall that it is God's style to defy the business conventions of corporate culture as we presently experience them. That is what he did in Jeremiah's day and with long-term success. (Again we are reminded of the

Theology of the Cross.) That God would still succeed when he goes against the grain is of course to be expected. After all, he owns the business, your business. And the sooner you get in line with the Boss (with God), the happier, the more fulfilling, your job will be.

No, tomorrow will not be just another Monday at your workplace. It can be a wonderful day for serving God. As you interact with your clients or co-workers, surf the Net, make your product, or clean the room, remember that you are God's mask for bringing good to the human community. You are a vehicle that God plans to use to express his love. Isn't your job a great one? It is filled with ultimate meaning and significance. Open your eyes, and you will see that (sometimes in a hidden way) you are doing God's work!

The founder of Methodism, John Wesley, put it so well once in a sermon:

> *3. Yet again: In what* spirit *do you go through your business? In the spirit of the world, or in the spirit of Christ? I am afraid thousands of those who are called good Christians do not understand the question. If you act in the spirit of Christ, you carry the end you at first proposed through all your work from the first to last. You do everything in the spirit of sacrifice, giving up your will to the will of God; and continually aiming, not at ease, pleasure, or riches, not of anything "this short-enduring world can give," but merely at the glory of God. Now, can any one deny, that this is the most excellent way of pursuing worldly business?*[10]

Wesley says that you are to give God the glory by giving everything you have on your job back to him and his people. Christian workers are people who finish what they start, who think of the customer, their co-workers, and God ahead of their needs. What a great way to do business! When you go against the grain of our current business ethos, and believe that God owns your business, it sets you free really to enjoy your job.

1. For these insights I am indebted to Stephen L. Carter, *The Culture of Disbelief* (New York: Basic Books, 1993), esp. pp. 3, 8-9.

2. Martin Luther, *Heidelberg Disputation* (1518), in *Luther's Works*, eds. Jaroslav Pelikan and Helmut T. Lehmann (55 vols.; Philadelphia and St. Louis: Fortress Press and Concordia Publishing House, 1955-1986), Vol. 31, p. 39.

3. *Ibid.*, p. 44.

4. Martin Luther, Commentary on Psalms, in *D. Martin Luthers Werke* (Weimarer Ausgabe) (56 vols.; Weimar: Hermann Böhlaus Nachfolger, 1883ff.), Vol. 40^{III}, pp. 370f.

5. See Richard Sennett, *The Corrosion of Character: The Personal Consequences of Work in the New Capitalism* (New York and London: W. W. Norton & Co., 1998), esp. pp. 96-97, 136-141.

6. Luther, "Commentary on Psalms," Vol. 40^{III}, p. 280.

7. Martin Luther, *Lectures on Deuteronomy* (1525/1526), in *Luther's Works*, Vol. 9, p. 96.

8. Karl Barth, *Church Dogmatics*, ed. G. W. Bromiley and T. F. Torrance (4 vols.: Edinburgh: T. & T. Clark, 1936-1962), Vol. III/4, p. 537.

9. *Catechism of the Catholic Church* (1994), p. 2426.

10. John Wesley, *The More Excellent Way* (n.d.), in *The Works of John Wesley* (14 vols.; 3rd ed.; Grand Rapids, Michigan: Baker Books, 1872), Vol. 7, p. 31.

Proper 22 • *Pentecost 20* • *Ordinary Time 27*

When Life Gets Hard, Christian, Rebel!

Lamentations 1:1-6

Jerusalem, the great capital, was in ruins. The Babylonians were in control. It was the beginning of the famed Babylonian Captivity. All the symbols of power, wealth, prestige, and influence were gone. No wonder so many Hebrews were in despair and that songs of lamentation like the one we just read as today's First Lesson were composed and long remembered.

Have you ever felt that way? Have you ever felt that life's moorings had been cut loose? Maybe it was the loss of a dear loved one, a child gone bad, a once-bright promising career destroyed by downsizing. Perhaps it has been a life lived without a special companion for whom you have yearned or a life lived in the depths of poverty and despair without hope. In those instances your heart has probably cried out just like the author of Lamentations did elsewhere:

> *See, O Lord, how distressed I am; my stomach churns, my heart is wrung within me....* — 1:20

> *All our enemies against us; panic and pitfall have come upon us, devastation and destruction....* — 3:46-47

> *The old men have left the city gate, the young men their music. The joy of our hearts has ceased; our dancing has been turned to mourning.* — 5:14-15

Have you ever felt those feelings? The book of Lamentations sheds profound light on how it feels when life gets hard. The book also calls our attention to what happens to people in societies when they are experiencing radical transition or deterioration — perhaps like ours. Hear these songs of lament: "All her people groan as they search for bread; they trade their treasures for food to revive their strength. Look, O Lord, and see how worthless I have become" (1:11).

People go begging for food in our society and all over the world. That does something to the human spirit. It makes the poor feel worthless. The lament continues: "Is it nothing to you, all you who pass by? Look and see if there is any sorrow like my sorrow ..." (1:12). Is that not the way we deal with the poor most of the time? We walk right on by.

The prison population in America grows daily, especially among African-American males. Long ago Lamentations prefigured this dynamic: "... behold my suffering; my young women and young men have gone into captivity" (1:18b).

Family life is deteriorating in our society. Civility and respect are increasingly in short supply. Authorities are challenged. Witness the guns and the shootings in American public schools. The ancient laments ring eerily in our ears:

> *We have become orphans, fatherless; our mothers, are like widows.* — 5:3

> *Slaves rule over us; there is no one to deliver us from their hand. We get our bread at the peril of our lives, because of the sword in the wilderness.* — 5:8-9

> *Women are raped ... virgins in the towns ... Princes are hung up by their hands; no respect is shown to the elders.* — 5:11-12

In a fundamental sense, times have not changed much. But is there no hope? Are we condemned merely to sing and live with the laments of Lamentations and Jeremiah? Can anything be done to set us free from all the hopelessness and despair? It will take a bunch of rebellious (Christian) malcontents.

Our other Bible lessons (2 Timothy 1:1-14; Luke 17:5-10) give some clues about the mental and emotional make-up of a Christian rebel. But there is another Old Testament book, one very much like Lamentations, which teaches us an important lesson about what it takes to be a Christian rebel. I am referring, of course, to the book of Ecclesiastes.

If Lamentations is a depressing book, Ecclesiastes is no less pessimistic about life. It begins with a song of lament about the vanity of life, that all we do has no ultimate significance because it ends up in a grave which is eventually forgotten by all of your heirs (1:1-11).

> *I hated all my toil in which I had toiled under the sun, seeing that I must leave it to those who come after me — and who knows whether they will be wise or foolish? Yet they will be master of all for which I toiled and used my wisdom under the sun. This also is vanity. So I turned and gave my heart up to despair concerning all the toil of my labors under the sun ... What do mortals get from all the toil and strain with which they toil under the sun? For all their days are full of pain, and their work is a vexation; even at night their minds do not rest. This also is vanity.* — 2:18-23

All life is unjust, the Preacher of Ecclesiastes laments. But it is especially unjust for the oppressed:

> *Again I saw all the oppressions that are practiced under the sun. Look, the tears of the oppressed — with no one to comfort them! On the side of their oppressors there was power — with no one to comfort them. And I thought the dead, who have already died, more fortunate than the living, who are still alive....* — 4:1-2

> *If you see in a province the oppression of the poor and the violation of justice and right, do not be amazed at the matter; for the high official is watched by a higher, and there are yet higher ones over them.* — 5:8

Ultimately life feels like an aimless chasing after wind.

What is a Christian to do in response to the hopelessness of the human condition? Where do we go from here?

Have you ever been as low on life as Lamentations and Ecclesiastes are? If not, you should be. These books are correct about the human condition since the Fall. With Lamentations we should be weeping over our condition (1:2a). We should be crying about the endless cycles of poverty and oppression, the destruction of people (3:48). And with Ecclesiastes we might lament as well over the aimlessness of life, recognizing its uselessness, because in the end all we do and the skills we develop are the result of one person envying another (4:4). It makes no difference anyway, because both the wise and the fool die, and both are forgotten. Life is indeed a vain chasing after wind (2:15-17).

I ask again: What can we Christians do when life gets hard, when we experience life like it really is? The logical answer is, "Nothing." Maybe suicide. It would be better had we never been born.

Heroically (or is it foolishly) the biblical witness does not surrender to this hopelessness and chaos. Ecclesiastes teaches us to go ahead and eat, drink, and enjoy our work (2:24). (Again we are reminded what a God-send work is.) "Go; eat your bread with enjoyment, and drink your wine with a merry heart ..." the Teacher of Ecclesiastes says (9:7a). Where does he get such courage? Both he and the author of Lamentations as well as all our assigned Bible lessons point us to a merciful, loving God as the source of such (rebellious) strength. We can eat with enjoyment and drink wine with a merry heart, the Teacher of Ecclesiastes says, because "God has long ago approved of what you do" (9:7). In Lamentations it is sung that:

> *The steadfast love of the Lord never ceases, his mercies never come to an end....*   — 3:22

> *For the Lord will not reject forever. Although he causes grief, he will have compassion according to the abundance of his steadfast love; for he does not willingly afflict or grieve anyone.*   — 3:31-33

In our Second Lesson (2 Timothy 1:8-10), Paul likewise claims that he could only endure his imprisonment for the Gospel because he could rely on the power of God's grace by which God called us before the foundation of the world. Faith in a loving God, even in small quantities, is a great, grand embolding thing. That is Jesus' point in his remarks about having faith the size of a mustard seed, in our Gospel Lesson (Luke 17:5-10).

When we break it down rationally, the "yes" that our Bible lessons say to life in the midst of all life's chaos and hard times does not make sense. That is hardly surprising given the paradoxical character of Christian faith. As usual the sixteenth-century reformer Martin Luther put it very well in one of his sermons. He wrote:

> *13. To this I reply: I have often said that feeling and faith are two different things. It is the nature of faith not to feel, to lay aside reason and close the eyes, to submit absolutely to the Word, and follow it in life and death. Feeling however does not extend beyond that which may be apprehended by reason and the senses, which may be heard, seen, felt, and known by the outward senses. For this cause feeling is opposed to faith and faith is opposed to feeling.*[1]

Christians are people who go against the grain, who rebel. When it becomes obvious to reason and experience that life is chaos, that it is harsh, that it is unjust and so we may as well submit to the powers that be, Christians say, "No," to these conclusions and work for justice and meaning in the world.

In describing the Christian life in this way I am reminded of reflections about being a rebel against injustice and chaos that the great French existentialist philosopher Albert Camus once uttered. Here's how he described our rebelliousness:

> *What is a rebel? A man who says no, but whose refusal does not imply a renunciation. He is also a man who says yes, from the moment he makes his first gesture of rebellion....*

> *In every act of rebellion, the rebel simultaneously experiences a feeling of revulsion at the infringement of his rights and a complete and spontaneous loyalty to certain aspects of himself. Thus he implicitly brings into play a standard of values....*[2]
>
> *Therefore the individual is not, in himself alone, the embodiment of values he wishes to defend. It needs all humanity, at least, to comprise them.*[3]

Camus himself was not a Christian, but he is clearly in touch with what is involved in Christian rebelliousness. Christians are people who say, "No," to the laws in life, to life's apparent meaninglessness, and to the oppression we encounter. They do not rebel for the sake of their own well-being, but for the sake of *all* their neighbors. In doing this, Christian rebels are counter-cultural. As Martin Luther King, Jr., said so many times, Christians are to be "maladjusted." Hear Dr. King tell it:

> *Every academic discipline has its technical nomenclature, and modern psychology has a word that is used, probably, more than any other. It is the word* maladjusted. *This word is a ringing cry of modern, child psychology. Certainly all of us want to live a well-adjusted life in order to avoid the neurotic personality. But I say to you, there are certain things within our social order to which I am proud to be maladjusted and to which I call upon all men of goodwill to be maladjusted....*
>
> *So let us be maladjusted, as maladjusted as the Prophet Amos, who in the midst of the injustices of his day could cry out in words that echo across the centuries, "Let justice run down like waters and righteousness like a mighty stream...." Let us be maladjusted as Jesus of Nazareth, who could look into the eyes of the men and women of his generation and cry out, "Love your enemies. Bless them that curse you. Pray for them that despitefully use you."*[4]

The next time life gets hard for you, the next time you chafe over injustice, rebel! In the Name of Christ, protest. Assert the meaningfulness of life through word and deed, even if you are not very sure of your ideals. Get in the trenches and work for justice (organize, protest), even if it looks like a lost cause.

Some people of goodwill rebel that way, but they don't stand a chance ultimately. You and I do not have the courage it takes to be "maladjusted" in Dr. King's sense. We can only do it, we only have the confidence and strength to do it, because of the power of faith (Luke 17:6).

Come to think of it, our faith in itself is not what gives the courage to rebel against the evils of life. It is the love of God that provides such courage, a confidence like Lamentations says in a God whose steadfast love never ceases (3:25), who does not willingly afflict or grieve us (3:33). With a loving God like that, the next time life gets hard and leads you to question life's meaning or the viability of seeking justice, Christians, you will not be able to stop yourself from rebelling. Christians are rebels, because we have a counter-cultural God who confounds the world's chaos! The chaos in your life is not God's will, and so the chaos and emptiness in life will not prevail!

---

1. Martin Luther, *Christ's Resurrection and Its Benefits* (n.d.), in *Sermons of Martin Luther*, ed. John Nicholas Lenker (8 vols.; reprint ed.; Grand Rapids, Michigan: Baker Book House, 1988), Vol. II, p. 224.

2. Albert Camus, *The Rebel*, trans. Anthony Bower (New York: Alfred A. Knopf, Inc., 1956), pp. 13-14.

3. *Ibid.*, p. 17.

4. Martin Luther King, Jr., *The American Dream* (1961), in *A Testament of Hope: The Essential Writings of Martin Luther King, Jr.*, ed. James M. Washington (San Francisco: Harper & Row, Publishers, 1986), pp. 215-216.

Proper 23 • *Pentecost 21* • *Ordinary Time 28*

In, But Not Of The World: A Spiritually Enriching, Liberating Experience

Jeremiah 29:1, 4-7

"What's important to me in my walk of faith is my relationship with God. Next comes my family. Christianity is about things of the spirit, not about the ways of the world." Many American Christians (perhaps some in this parish) feel this way. How about you? Does a Christian have a responsibility for society? Should the Church play a role in trying to turn American society around?

Let me try to answer those questions by asking you a question. Do you believe what the Bible teaches? If so, let's see what our First Lesson from the book of Jeremiah proclaims.

The text we are considering from Jeremiah for this Sunday is part of a letter written after Jerusalem had fallen to the Babylonians, and many Hebrews had been sent into exile in the foreign land of Babylon. Life for these exiles was not excessively harsh. They were not prisoners of war, but were allowed to meet and confer freely. They were treated like resident aliens. (Our lesson from Jeremiah implies this [vv.4-7].)[1]

The life of the Jewish exiles in Babylon might even be compared to the status of Christians in the world. They (we) live *in* the world, but are not really *of* the world (John 17:14-16). That is precisely the point. This text, written to the Babylonian exiles who were both residents of Babylon, but not *of* that empire, is a text that speaks directly to us Christians. We share with the ancient Hebrew Babylonian exiles a very similar situation.

Essentially Jeremiah wrote to the leaders of the exiles to tell them that they needed to make plans to stay in Babylon a long time. (Apparently they had heard from others that they could expect a speedy return home to Judah [Jeremiah 27:14].) We Christians have been dwelling in this "foreign land" of ours for nearly 2,000 years; Christ's Second Coming to bring us "home" to the fully-realized Kingdom of God does not seem to be something that is going to happen soon. Like the Hebrew exiles in Babylon. we need to build our homes in the world, make arrangements to support ourselves, and think about the possibility of our sons and daughters marrying outside the Christian family (Jeremiah 29:5-7).

All right, these are the sorts of things you do when you are a resident-alien in a foreign land. However, God had Jeremiah give the Hebrew exiles and us Christians some advice that really blows your mind. Listen to the actual words of Jeremiah, as God gave them to him. They are spoken to you: "But seek the welfare of the city where I have sent you into exile, and pray to the Lord on its behalf, for in its welfare you will find your welfare" (v. 7).

Work for the welfare of the city in which you find yourself, and pray on behalf of that city. In one sense this does not seem like very sensible advice. It certainly must have gone against the grain of the Hebrew exiles. After all, for them the one place on earth where God had decreed them to live was Israel. The one place where God dwelt was there (in the Temple in Jerusalem). But now they were being told to redefine these religious commitments. They were directed to seek God and serve him in new territory, not on sacred turf, but in the secular realm.

In this Bible lesson is God asking you and me to redefine our Christian commitments too? He seems to be telling us that, although as Christians our real home is in the things of the Spirit, we not only need to live in the world, but we will also have some of our richest spiritual experiences and opportunities to participate in God's liberating work, in worldly moments. The Church is not the only place for spirituality and for hearing God's freeing Word. Let us carefully reconsider Jeremiah's words in order to see very clearly how spiritual our immersion in worldly affairs can be.

First, note that Jeremiah wants the Hebrew exiles and us to *pray* on behalf of the welfare of the world. Praying for yourself or just for your friends is selfish prayer. To pray for others, especially those who take no account of our wishes or our rights, is a powerful antidote to combat our selfishness, which is the essence of sin.[2] Prayer for others, especially for those not of the family of faith, helps us crucify our sin, and so is a wonderful occasion for practicing the Christian life!

Remember that Paul teaches in Romans 6 that in our baptism the old self filled with sin has been crucified so that our new Christlike self could rise (or emerge). Christian life involves living this baptismal experience — saying, "No," to your sinful selfish self in order to rise to a life full of Christ and your neighbor. That denying of yourself and your selfish desire begins to happen when you pray for others, especially for others who do not belong to you or are not part of your kin. In such prayer you put God and the welfare of God's creatures ahead of yourself.

That is a very freeing experience, when you are not so hung up on yourself that you come to care about God and others. At those times your personal anxieties are not so binding as they used to be; you are a little freer. Living fully in the world, caring for it so much that you pray for it, is an opportunity for enriching your spiritual life, for living out the self-denying lifestyle that your baptism lures you to embrace.

To this juncture I have been talking more about what being in and not of the world can do for you and me as individuals. But the kind of lifestyle that Jeremiah and I are extolling can do a lot for the *world*, and for our community, too.

The sixteenth-century founder of Lutheranism, Martin Luther, went so far as to say that Christians keep the world afloat. In a sermon in 1537, he put it this way:

> ... *in both the spiritual and the temporal realms the very greatest works in the world — even though they are not recognized and acknowledged as such — are continually performed by Christians ... Consequently, the Christians are genuine saviors, yes, lords and gods of the world ... God does not want it forgotten that whatever possessions and power the world has it holds in fee from the beggars described by St. Paul (2 Corinthians*

6:19) "as having nothing, and yet possessing everything." Everything that God grants the world he gives because of Christians.[3]

I am not sure that I agree entirely with Luther at this point. There are plenty of non-Christians who contribute profoundly to our world and to the well-being of our community. However, the reformer has a real point in calling attention to the contributions that we Christians can and do make to society. We do it through our prayers.

We have been talking about that. As we try to bring the Good News of Jesus to the world so that the world may be saved, we also make a contribution to the world. Our Second Lesson makes this point, claiming that this concern is what kept Saint Paul going (2 Timothy 2:10). The Christian contribution to the world also surfaces in less clearly spiritual, more worldly ways. When you get to work tomorrow, you have a great opportunity to contribute to society. You do that by undertaking your job to serve the whole human community. Work in that spirit, doing it to glorify God, and you will be making a profound contribution to the world. We have previously talked about this. (See the sermon for Proper 21.)

We Christians can also contribute to the welfare of the world in a very special way by virtue of our status of being in, but not of the world. Because we are aliens in the world, sort of like those exiles in Babylon to whom Jeremiah wrote, we may be less prone to work only for ourselves. After all, as aliens we can never make the world our own, just as a Hebrew could never have become the Babylonian Emperor. To the degree that we don't get sucked into the world, and keep on being Christian in our outlook, we will not so readily get lured into the world's power games. Society needs people like that. A community's health depends on some checking of individual egoism in order to comprehend the interests of others and enlarge areas of cooperation.[4]

Think of that when you drive home. Road safety depends on drivers suppressing their egotistical desires (to get home quickly) in interests of the greater good (road safety for everyone). I need to stop at that red light in order to protect everyone's safety, even though my ego tells me to run that light so I can get home sooner. Society needs people who will not get into ego satisfaction at the expense of the good of the whole. Christians are people who, when they live their faith, will say, "No," to themselves for the sake of their neighbor. We are like those Hebrew exiles in Babylon called to forego a narrow focus on returning home to Israel in order to seek to enhance the welfare of the land in which they were living (Jeremiah 29:7).

The world, American society, is certainly caught up in self-seeking, in the quest for self-fulfilment. It is why the family structure and other moral standards are breaking down. There is a sense in which all societies are rooted in or held together by such self-seeking. When it gets out of hand, though, Christians and their Church need to get their hands dirty in social and political movements, advocating and witnessing to an alternative lifestyle — to a life that does not care about self-fulfilment or power. That is the kind of lifestyle to which Jeremiah is calling you.

Work for the good of society as a whole, not just for yourself or your own group. Seek the fellowship with all human beings for which Martin Luther King, Jr., called, one beyond your race, tribe, class, and nation. Be like an apple tree that Martin Luther wants Christians to emulate, one that offers its fruit to everyone, even to swines.[5]

Christian, get your hands dirty in the affairs of society and of your community. Get out of this building, out of your family and network of friends and coworkers, then go and serve! This church needs to become more active in this community, to support community organizations, for the same reason. The world is depending on us. It needs more people who do not give into themselves and their egos.

Are Jeremiah and I asking you to forego the spiritual quest, to put them on the back-burner for the sake of worldly pursuits? No way. We ask you to be in the world, not of it. Get in the world, but don't do the world's egocentric "thing."

An ancient African theologian, Augustine, says that when you get into community affairs in a selfless loving way, trying not to feed your ego, you will see God more clearly than if you had not.

Because God is love, if you do not have a self-emptying agape love for all your neighbors, you will not recognize God when he comes to you. But when you do practice loving all God's people, you must love love itself, and because God is love, loving God's people will make you love God more.[6] Again it is obvious how and why getting involved, getting this church involved in the affairs of the world, can facilitate a closer walk with God.

Of course I do not want to give you the wrong impression. You and I cannot *make* ourselves live the sort of in, but not of the world lifestyle about which Jeremiah speaks. On our own we cannot live the baptismal life that involves the daily crucifixion of sin and selfishness and the freedom that comes from living for all our neighbors and for Christ. Those things only happen because God makes them happen to us. Remember you did not baptize yourself; God did it. The ancient Hebrews who lived in, but not of the world (of the Babylonian Empire) did not place themselves in that situation. It was all God's decision and work that brought them to Babylon. Likewise it is the same with you and me and our efforts to live in but not of the world. God puts us in that situation.

The vision of Christian life that Jeremiah and I have extolled in this sermon has not been a demand that you start living differently. We have just been describing who you already are. You see, Christians, you are not *of* this world. But you are *in* it. You may as well be yourself, be the person you are. This world is not really what you want. You'll only be happy, only be true to the "you" that God has made you to be, when you live a life *for* the world (a life dedicated to making things better in the world).

No, Jeremiah and I as God's mouthpieces and puppets are not telling you what you must do. You are too free for more rules. We just want you to be aware of the situation in which God has placed you, as a creature who is in and not of the world. When you recognize that you do not have a real stake in the things of the world except to see it as an opportunity to love God by loving his creatures and the things he has made, you will not be able to stop showering love and compassion on the world and its creatures. You will do all that for the glory of God. Being in the world, engaging in activities that can help the world, is a fulfilling, liberating, spiritual experience that will make God more real in your life. Christians, get out of here and get in the community, in the world, where you belong!

---

1. G. W. Anderson, *The History and Religion of Israel* (London: Oxford University Press, 1966), p. 141.

2. For this insight I am indebted to Dietrich Bonhoeffer, *Letters and Papers from Prison,* ed. Eberhard Bethge (New York: The Macmillan Co., 1968), p. 160.

3. Martin Luther, *Sermons on the Gospel of John* (1537), in *Luther's Works,* Vol. 24, p. 82.

4. For an elaboration of these themes, see Reinhold Niebuhr, *Moral Men and Immoral Society* (New York: Charles Scribner's Sons, 1932), pp. 274-276.

5. Martin Luther King, Jr., *Where Do We Go From Here: Chaos or Community?* (New York: Harper & Row, 1967); Martin Luther, *Sermons of 1532,* in *Weimar Ausgabe,* Vol. 36, pp. 456-457.

6. Augustine, *Homilies on the First Letter of John* (415), IX.10-11.

Proper 24 • *Pentecost 22* • *Ordinary Time 29*

Your Sins Are Remembered No More; You're Free!

Jeremiah 31:27-34

Have you ever felt weighed down by your sins and shortcomings? Have you ever despaired over your ability to live up to expectations — God's expectations, society's expectations, your own self-expectations? Do you wish that you could have a fresh start? The Prophet Jeremiah was proclaiming a Word to sinful, insecure people like us, to people whose confidence in the future had been badly shaken.

Have you ever made a big mistake in your life, a mistake for which you paid for many years? Maybe you are still paying for those mistakes. That was the situation of the ancient Hebrews in Jeremiah's day. They were a conquered people, both the Northern Kingdom of Israel (by Assyria) and the Southern Kingdom of Judah (by the Babylonians). They had come to understand their present political plight as a consequence of their sin (Jeremiah 2; 25:1-14).[1]

When you are in a mess, when life is not turning out as you had hoped it would, and you feel that it is your fault, life can be a living hell. The memories of what you have done wrong to put yourself in the situation you are in do not die. They are brought to the fore daily. Perhaps you are still making those same mistakes.

For the addict who has lost family, job, and hope because of that addiction, the sins of the past are still alive. The patterns of addiction continue. The partners in a shattered marriage relationship, one destroyed by selfish behavior and a failure to forgive, are still living with the consequences of such behavior. So are their children. Neglectful parents and their children bear the scars of such parental neglect. Our nation still bears the scars of our earlier behaviors, of slavery and of sexism. (Those behaviors are still transpiring.)

How is it with you? Have I named any of the "exiles" in which you find yourself? Are you castigating yourself for any of these indiscretions? Do they explain your present unhappiness? I certainly have named one, when I spoke of the scars of slavery and sexism. These social maladies plague our nation, and so they plague you and me to this very day.

All of us are plagued by our mistakes of the past in our spiritual lives. Who of us here today has no spiritual flaws, no doubts, no skeletons in the closet? Certainly I am not innocent. Old sloppy habits of prayer (or the lack of it), regrets about moral lapses (many when we were younger), have a way of haunting you in later years.

We really are "hurting dudes." Like the Hebrew exiles we are a long way from home (from where we should be in life). This community, this nation, you and I are haunted by mistakes of the past. In ministering to our despair, God has Jeremiah tell us about a fresh start he is going to give us, a new covenant that he will create (Jeremiah 31:31). And in that new covenant, the one that we Christians believe has been instituted by Christ, God will forgive our iniquity and remember our sin no more (v. 34)! God no longer remembers the sin that you and I commit. He remembers your failures no more.

Forgiveness is a beautiful reality. Its dictionary meaning connotes pardon and giving up resentment. In the languages in which the Bible was written, Hebrew and Greek, forgiveness literally means "sending away" (*aphesis* and *selichah*) or "lifting away" (*nasa*) and "covering" (*kaphar*). Our mistakes and sins are sent away or covered. Is that not what happens when you are forgiven? Your mistakes do not count anymore; they are pardoned or overlooked.

Jeremiah adds one other nuance in our First Lesson. Yahweh says that he will remember our sin no more (v. 34). The errors of the past are forgotten and forgiven.

Forgive and forget. Can you really do it? Of course we forgive the wrongs done to us. That is the Christian way. But do you really forget the indiscretion? Do you not keep your eye on the one you forgave, just in case, even if you sincerely forgave them? On this side of the Fall into sin, only a "rube" acts like the indiscretion done to you did not happen. Even when you forgive yourself for a bad decision or a bad habit, you do not forget it. Your memories are scarred by it. That is precisely why you and I, why our society, is in such bondage. We cannot get past our bad memories.

Oh, but that is not the way that God forgives. He wipes the slate clean! God remembers your sin and my sin no more. We really are forgiven. Our sins are forgotten!

Can you feel how freeing this Word is? The sins of the past, the misdeeds of the past, and the bad habits that may still be plaguing you, God has forgotten them. And if God has forgotten them, all those wrongs do not have ultimate meaning any more. They have no eternal significance. If God has forgotten them, perhaps you and I can too.

What a liberating Word! All the burdens which have worn you down, all the regrets, all the suspicions, all the bad habits do not count anymore. They do not exist in the memory of God.

Think of it: When you forget something, it no longer exists for you. An ancestor forgotten, remembered by no one, no longer exerts a meaningful impact among the living. A great recipe forgotten no longer can make mealtime better. A friend forgotten is no longer a friend (and never really was). And a pain which is forgotten is no longer painful.

That is the way our sins are with God. All the things that have caused you pain, all the dead ends you have had in your life, they do not exist for God anymore. They do not exist, because they were not made by God, and so we might say that they and all sin are "non-being," nothingness.[2] Why, then, do you keep on clinging to the bad memories of the past, to the regrets, to the suspicions, to the bad habits? God has forgotten them; you can too!

Are you concerned about what other people or what society says about you, what your image in the community is? That does not matter either. God does not count such views. He has forgotten them along with the sins you have committed.

What a freeing Word! All the behaviors and memories or the slanderous impressions others have of you, that have held you captive, no longer matter. Even more glorious is that we do not have to do anything to earn this kind of forgiveness. It is a free gift of God!

I could just end the sermon at this point, and let you reflect on the goodness of God, and how his love for you has set you free from all the old claims that have enslaved you. But Jeremiah did not stop at that point, and so I will not either.

Besides proclaiming that God would no longer remember the Hebrews' and our sin in God's Name, Jeremiah also proclaimed that the new covenant made by Yahweh would be one in which he would put his Law within us, write it in our hearts. What does this have to do with you and me and God's blessed forgetfulness?

Sometimes when God's forgiving love gets stressed, people say that it just encourages permissiveness. Such people claim that too much stress on God forgetting our sin may send a message that we can go out and sin, since it will be forgiven anyway. The sixteenth-century reformer Martin Luther had a great response. He wrote:

> *For our sins are not forgiven with the design that we should continue to commit sin, but that we should cease from it. Otherwise it would more justly be called, not forgiveness of sin, but permission to sin.*[3]

Jeremiah's reflections on the Law that God has written in our hearts serve to underline Luther's claim that God's forgiveness has not given us permission to sin. "But wait a minute," you say. "I thought that forgiveness was by grace, that we are free from the Law" (see Galatians 3:10-12).

Recall that Jeremiah is talking about a new covenant, which we Christians believe is fulfilled in Jesus Christ. Do not forget what Jesus says about the Law of God. He claims that he did not come to abolish the Law, but to fulfill it (Matthew 5:17-19). If Jesus fulfils the Law, and we are to read Jeremiah as pointing to Christ, then when Jeremiah says that God will put his Law in us, this must also be seen as a prophecy of what will happen to us in Christ. To say that God puts the Law in us, and since the Law is fulfilled by Christ, it seems that we can read our First Lesson as a prophecy of Christ (the fulfillment of the Law) living in us.

The New Testament refers to Christ taking up residence in the believer. Paul says that Christ is within him (Galatians 2:20), that Christ dwells in our hearts (Ephesians 3:17). Martin Luther picked up this theme to explain why salvation by grace does not lead to a lackadaisical attitude to Christian living. He spoke of Christ living in us, so intimately that Christ and our conscience become one. Living in us, Christ abolishes the demands of the Law along with sin and death, just as he did on the Cross. All the evils that torment and afflict us are absorbed by him.

Of course when Christ comes and lives in us he comes with all the marvelous characteristics he has. He brings to us his grace, his righteousness, and his perfection in fulfilling God's Law. Those good qualities become part of us, part of who we are.[4] Get that, Christ's fulfillment of the Law lives in you, Christian. In that sense, the Law of God is within you, written on your heart.

Elsewhere Luther calls this relationship that believers have with Jesus when they are saved (justified) by grace the "blessed exchange." His words are powerful and often quoted. Here is how he put it:

> *The third incomparable benefit of faith is that it unites the soul with Christ as a bride is united with her bridegroom. By this mystery, as the Apostle teaches, Christ and the soul become one flesh [Ephesians 5:31-32]. And if they are one flesh and there is between them a true marriage — indeed the most perfect of all marriages, since human marriages are but poor examples of this one true marriage — it follows that everything they have they hold in common, the good as well as the evil. Accordingly the believing soul can boast of and glory in whatever Christ has as though it were its own, and whatever the soul has Christ claims as His own.*[5]

Luther says that when we are forgiven by God (justified by grace) it is like getting married to Jesus. In a good marriage the partners share everything in common. Those of you who have been happily married have some sense of how the "blessed exchange," the sharing that goes on between spouses, changes lives. The lovers in a long-time relationship are not the same persons they were when they first fell in love. Could you say that love has made them forget themselves? That is God's style for setting us free and changing lives.

I have a friend who talks of his marriage this way. He says that after 27 years of life together with his wife, sometimes he catches himself thinking or acting in ways he never did before they met nearly three decades ago. He says that when he thinks more about those behaviors, he realizes that his new cautiousness is really an emulation of her style. Not that he is really imitating his wife self-consciously, but he says that he can see her style and thought patterns in what he is doing. It is not "her" style that he is embodying in those instances. It is now he. Her style has rubbed off on him.

Likewise when he observes his wife's style in recent years, he notes that she is not always so cautious in expressing herself as she was typically. Sometimes she speaks her mind publicly. It is almost like he can see himself in her in those instances. But his wife is not imitating him. It is just that some of his qualities have begun to get in her blood. Close human relationships work that way. They change us.

We return now to the idea that we have been married to Jesus in faith. This is the new covenant about which Jeremiah spoke. God has written his Law on our hearts by wedding us to his Son, the One who perfectly fulfilled the Law. Jesus' characteristics, his righteousness, his love and his ability to fulfill the Law, are rubbing off on you and me.

How long have you been a Christian? How long have you known Jesus? Over the years his passion for the Law has gotten to you. Just as he fulfills the Law without anybody having to teach him how to do it, so you and I have the Law in our guts. The real you and me who want to please Jesus, our divine spouse, also love keeping God's commands. Jeremiah promised it would happen.

Remember that I talked about how good marriage relationships change you? It is obvious that our new covenant relationship with the Messiah, getting married to Jesus, changes us. The sinner in me hates the Law. I am selfish and want to do my thing. But in that marriage with Jesus, now the Law is in me, who I am.

Sometimes when I think of my marriage, I am so changed that I have almost forgotten who I was before my wife and I met. God's love is more powerful than that. He not only forgives our sin and changes you and me so much that we can hardly remember who we were before He came into our lives, but also he even forgot the old destructive way we used to be.

Is not God's love breathtaking? In forgetting our sin, the Lord sets you and me free. He changes us so much that we begin to forget the old self-destructive people we used to be. Remember that new covenant word the next time that you are depressed about life, friends. The old behaviors and attitudes that have haunted you are remembered no more. As you get wrapped up in Jesus' life, in the relationship he has with you and as his Law gets written on your heart, you will begin to forget the old wounds and destructive behaviors too. God's love truly is miraculous! It sets us free from what has been haunting our lives.

---

1. There is much scholarly debate over whether the prophecy in the First Lesson and others in Chapters 30-33 were directed to Israel or to Judah. Many scholars believe that subsequent editing led to the application of these prophecies to both. See Claus Westermann, *Handbook to the Old Testament*, trans. and ed. Robert H. Boyd (Minneapolis: Augsburg Publishing House, 1976), pp. 164-165; Brevard S. Childs, *Introduction to the Old Testament as Scripture* (Philadelphia: Fortress Press, 1979), pp. 350-352, 353-354. Childs' reflections imply that insofar as the process of composition of the book of Jeremiah may have involved revising Jeremiah's original prophecy to apply to another situation, so what I am doing in this sermon, applying Jeremiah's prophecy to twenty-first-century Christians, is appropriate.

2. For this idea of sin as nothingness, I am indebted to Karl Barth, *Church Dogmatics*, Vol. IV/1, pp. 408ff.

3. Martin Luther, *Exhortation to Live in the Spirit Since We Have Become the Children of God, Sons and Heirs* (n.d.), in *Sermons of Martin Luther*, Vol. VIII, pp. 168-169.

4. Martin Luther, *Lectures on Galatians* (1531/1535), in *Luther's Works*, Vol. 26, pp. 166-168.

5. Martin Luther, *The Freedom of a Christian* (1520), in *Luther's Works*, Vol. 31, p. 351.

Proper 25 • Pentecost 23 • Ordinary Time 30

A Fresh Start!

Joel 2:23-32

Have you ever felt that you were absolutely at the end of your rope, left without hope? Sometime during the years of 539 B.C. to 331 B.C. that is the way the people of Judah felt. It seems that their land had been ravaged by a plague of locusts which had had catastrophic consequences.

Once a harvest has been destroyed, you cannot repair it. If a building has burned to the ground, you cannot repair it. In those instances you need to start from scratch with a fresh start.

Have you reached the end of your rope? Are all your options closed? Is there no more hope for a happy, meaningful life for you? Are all the career options closed? Is the family relationship shattered? Has our cynicism about government reached a point where confidence in our system is irretrievable? Have the moral and educational standards of our society forever eroded? If you answered, "Yes," to any of those questions you have come to a dead-end. That is the way that the people of Judah whom the Prophet Joel addressed felt. The locust plague had produced among them and their nation a state of chaos and the sense of hopelessness one feels in the midst of poverty or when there seems to be no way out.

Consider the way the rural poor with no land, an urban resident of the projects short on education, or the homeless must feel about their prospects for the future. Think about how you felt or feel those times when all the options seem closed. Are you in touch with those feelings? If so, you know how the people of Judah whom Joel addressed felt.

What did Joel say to them? What does he say to us and to those without hope in our society? First Joel told the Judeans and us to lament for our situation, to repent, and to worship (Joel 1:13-14). (Joel himself was apparently a great advocate of Temple worship in Jerusalem and its cult of sacrifice.) Joel's point, like those of most Old Testament prophets, was that what was going wrong for the Hebrews was in some sense their own fault. They had sinned, like you and I sin.

"Wait," you say. "Is it really the case that whenever something goes wrong for people in life it is their fault? Are the worst, sinful people the ones who suffer?" Not quite. You are thinking more individualistically than the ancient Hebrews did. They thought more in terms of the community. Consequently when the prophets like Joel claim that the evils which had befallen the Hebrews or were to happen were the punishments for their sin, individuals are not typically singled out. The charge that sin is the cause of the locust plague and the other tragedies that had befallen Judah pertains to all the people. Their collective sin had brought about the catastrophe on all of them.

Collective sin: This is the sense in which we can agree with Joel and the other Old Testament prophets that the bad things in life, that the "dead ends" we encounter, are our own fault. If there had not been a Fall into sin, would work be the chore that it is for many (Genesis 3:17b-19)? Perhaps there would be no sexism and other forms of discrimination (Genesis 3:16). Could it be, ladies, that even the birth process would be easier (Genesis 3:16a)? Certainly life would not be filled with the anxiety and despair it often is (Romans 7:14-23; Ecclesiastes).

Think about it. Was it God's original plan for there to be death, sickness, suffering, and catastrophes? No, God made the world good (Genesis 1:4, 10, 12, 18, 21, 25). Consequently, all the suffering, death, and natural catastrophes we experience must not be what God wants, but are the result of or reactions to sin, which has destroyed the original harmony between the created order and God. In that sense Joel and the prophets are correct: The evils we encounter in life are a consequence of sin.

Do not think that you are off the hook because you can blame our less-than-perfect world on the sins of others, like Adam and Eve. You and I are sinning too. Any perfect people here? Insofar as you and I keep on sinning, do what we do to satisfy our own egos and not what our neighbors need, we are contributing to all the problems in the world. In that sense, the problems in your life and in mine, the hopeless situations that you and I are in, or have been in, are our own fault. Like the people of Judah whom Joel addressed, the mess that we are in is a consequence of our sin. Like them, we need a fresh start. Hear how God told Joel he would give it to the Judeans and to us.

Joel proceeded next to reiterate his call to repentance and suggested that the locust plague would get worse. Some biblical scholars speculate that his references in chapter 2 (vv. 4-5), just before our assigned lesson starts, to a plague of locusts really refers to an army from the north which Joel believed would invade Judah and result in a catastrophic Day of Judgment.[1] Whether this is the case or not, the way in which Joel proceeded from the first crisis of the locust plague to an even worse one which raised apprehensions that the end of the world was coming is typical of the way most people respond to crises in life.

Is that not the way life goes sometimes? We encounter a problem, seem to solve it, and then it gets worse, so bad that there seems no way out. That is how it was for the people Joel addressed. They truly were at the end of their rope. A tragic end seemed inevitable.

Have you ever been there? Have you ever reached a point in your life when you felt that there was little point in going on? Perhaps it was the end of a relationship, the loss of a job, the death of a loved one, a debilitating illness. There was no way out. You had nowhere to turn and no other options to explore, and you realized that you bore responsibility for your plight. Your only hope was a fresh start.

Some observers who lament the present state of American society reflect that kind of despair. The system no longer works, they say. Trust is gone; standards are lost. Are we coming to the End Times, if not the end of America as we have known it? If you have felt such feelings or are feeling them now, then you know how it was for the Hebrews whom Joel addressed. His words may be for you.

What did Joel say next? Again he calls his hearers and us to repentance, to a recognition that the evil we encounter is our fault (2:12-17). This time, though, this call is linked to the portrait of God as a God of love, One who is: " ... gracious and merciful, slow to anger, and abounding in steadfast love ... (2:13b). A God like that One, so full of love, is a God who inspires repentance. The steadfast love of our God so overflows that it permeates our lives and changes them. As Martin Luther once put it, "The love of God which lives in man loves sinners, evil persons, fools, and weaklings in order to make them righteous, good, wise, and strong. Rather than seeking its own good, the love of God flows forth and bestows good."[2] God's love makes stubborn people, like those of us at the end of our rope, repent.

Joel proceeded next to account all the great things that this loving God would do for the people of Judah. It is not unlike what he plans to do for you and me and for our society. He said, in the Name of the Lord, that the army of the north would withdraw and that the locust plague would end too (2:18-25). The people of Judah, it was claimed, would be satisfied, enjoy prosperity, and never again be put to shame (v. 26).

But things do not get back to normal that easily or simply when you have come to the end of your rope. Something radically new has to happen. You have to get free, because when you hit rock bottom you have been in bondage, and the scars of such bondage do not vanish without a radical change. You can see that in our society, in how those segments of American society which have been most oppressed bear the scars of that oppression. It is why there is such a high percentage of the impoverished and African-American males in prison, why alcoholism rates are so high among Native Americans, and why women of impoverished classes have a higher percentage of out-of-wedlock births. Today's children of divorce tend to have less confidence about the future.[3] The oppressed, those who have been hurt, need a radically new beginning, a fresh start. You and I need that fresh start.

Joel knew that we all need a fresh start. This is why he related the promise of restoration for Judah to the Day of the Lord, to the End of Time (2:1). He proceeds to describe what God will do on the last Day of the Lord. This brings me to the punch-line of this sermon. Let me read you Joel's account of God's promise:

> *Then afterward I will pour out my spirit on all flesh; your sons and your daughters shall prophesy, your old men shall dream dreams, and your young men shall see visions. Even on the male and female slaves, in those days, I will pour out my spirit.* — 2:28-29

Our First Lesson continues with the blessed assurance that in this Last Day everyone who calls on the Name of the Lord shall be saved (v. 32).

What does this reference to the gift of the Holy Spirit have to do with the End Times and what do both have to do with the fresh start we need? This very passage makes us think of Pentecost, when the Holy Spirit was first poured out on the Church. In fact in Peter's sermon on that occasion he even quoted these verses from our First Lesson from Joel (Acts 2:16-21). For the earliest Christians this gift of the Holy Spirit was seen as a sign that the End Times had come, and this association of the outpouring of the Spirit with the End was related both to Jesus' preaching that the End was upon us (Mark 1:15) and to the book of Joel's identification of the two.

So what? What does the End Times have to do with us, when they are so far off in the future? Since the End has not come for two millennia, maybe it will never come. Besides what does this have to do with me in facing my problems?

Joel's identification of the gift of the Holy Spirit with the End Times speaks directly to our need for a fresh start, as individuals and as a nation. Before Joel's prophecy and its Christian fulfillment, some Hebrews — its leaders and prophets — received the Spirit (Exodus 31:3; 35:31; Judges 3:10; 1 Samuel 11:6; 16:3; Ezekiel 3:12,14). But Joel saw that what would be different at the End was that the Spirit would be poured out on all.

I ask you church members, do you have the Holy Spirit? Has it been poured out on you? Do not look for the Spirit under that pew. All of you who are baptized have the Holy Spirit. Paul says that in 1 Corinthians 12:13. The Spirit has been poured out on all of us, the old and the young, male and female. Joel says that that must mean the End has come (2:28-29). We are in the End Times! Believe it, friends. (The technical term for this belief is "realized eschatology.")

What does this mean for us in our daily lives, trying to cope with all the dead ends we and our society face? Being in the End Times as we are, you and I have the fresh start that we need! The old has passed away, and everything is new. Paul says that in 2 Corinthians (5:17). How does the Holy Spirit figure in this?

Those of us who have been crippled by the past, with no viable alternatives, have been in bondage to our past, trapped by who and what we are. The impoverished segments of society have been enslaved by the past. But the Good News of Joel and his message about the End Time is that we are no longer chained by our pasts. The Holy Spirit is the agent of the new possibilities, by giving us the faith that throws off the old dead ends in favor of embracing the new creatures that Christ is creating in you and me (Ephesians 4:22-24).

The greatest Reformed theologian of our century, a Swiss German ethnic named Karl Barth, offered a profound insight about the Holy Spirit. In his view, "to have the Spirit, to live in the Spirit means being set free and being permitted to live in freedom."[4] Freedom is precisely what a person and society who have run out of options do not have. At the end of your rope, you have no options.

In what sense does the Spirit set us free? Again, Karl Barth has a definition of freedom that is profound. "Freedom," he says, "means being in spontaneous and therefore willing agreement with the sovereign freedom of God."[5] You are not really free, Barth seems to claim, when you seek yourself. You need to get free from yourself (since it is your sin that has gotten you in your problematic situation). You are only really free from those old destructive patterns when you *want* to do God's Will, and the Holy Spirit is the One who makes you want what God wants.

Do you get the point? Those of us trapped by our pasts, at the end of our ropes, are trapped by our own life circumstances and behavior. Only with a fresh start can we get free, and the only way that will happen is if we get free from ourselves and get wrapped up in God's ways. The Holy Spirit is God grabbing hold of us in such a way that doing God's thing is what we really want. When the Holy Spirit grabs you, it is a whole new way of living (God's Way), a fresh start.

Of course there is still a temptation for those of us set free to go back to the old destructive ways which led us to a dead end. We cannot avoid the lure of these old habits. Here the Holy Spirit is our Comforter. The founder of Methodism, John Wesley says all that needs to be said about the matter. In a 1736 sermon, he wrote:

> *... but the light that most necessarily attends to it [the Holy Spirit] is a light to discern the fallacies of flesh and blood, to reject the irreligious maxims of the world, and to practise those degrees of trust in God and love to men, whose foundation is not so much the present appearances of things, as in some that are yet to come. The object which this light brings us most immediately to know is ourselves....*[6]

The Holy Spirit keeps you from falling back into bondage by getting you in touch with the brand new creature that God has made you to be. Like Joel says, friends, take heart! The new day has come. You are free from the old chains that bound you, free to be the real (new) you and to find your true freedom serving God. And in that freedom you will want to work to abolish every prejudice and structure that oppresses. After all, Joel said in our lesson that all who call on God shall be delivered (v. 32). That means (according to Martin Luther) that "there will be no distinction either of places or of persons."[7] The fresh start, the freedom that the Spirit gives, is a Word of liberation for all! God has given you and me and all those who have gotten the shaft in life a fresh start. He has set us free (to do his thing).

1. Among scholars arguing this point include H. W. Wolff, *Die Botschaft des Joel* (Munich, 1963).

2. Martin Luther, *Heidelberg Disputation* (1518), in *Luther's Works*, Vol. 31, p. 57.

3. For these statistics or assessments, see Andrew Hacker, *Two Nations: Black and White, Separate, Hostile, Unequal* (New York: Ballantine Books, 1992/1995), pp. 90, 204; Allan Bloom, *The Closing of the American Mind* (New York: Simon and Schuster, 1987), pp. 120-121.

4. Karl Barth, *Dogmatics in Outline*, trans. G. T. Thomson (reprint ed.; New York: Harper & Row, 1959), p. 138.

5. Barth, *Church Dogmatics*, Vol. IV/1, p. 201.

6. John Wesley, *On Holy Spirit* (1736), in *The Works of John Wesley*, Vol. 7, pp. 514-515.

7. Martin Luther, *Lectures on Joel* (1524), in *Luther's Works,* Vol. 18, p. 112.

Proper 26 • *Pentecost 24* • *Ordinary Time 31*

Life's Not Always Fair: But God Will Straighten It Out!

Habakkuk 1:1-4; 2:1-4

Those of us who are old enough and socially concerned enough recall the 1960s with fondness. Troubled as the times were, it was a hopeful decade, a period when many of us dreamed that better days were on the horizon. We sang and dreamed of love and peace. We thought that the Civil Rights movement would put an end to racism, that the war on poverty might be won.

Today, nearly half a century later, those battles have not been won. The rich are getting richer; the poor are getting poorer; money from special interests buys elections; racism, prejudice, and sexism, have not been set aside. What has happened to our dreams?

In a sense the hopes and dreams of a just society do not even stir most Americans any longer. Those old hopes and dreams are said to represent the values of those "liberals" who are out of step with what America wants and is really like. Some even say that such dreams contradict basic Christian values. Besides we are too busy to address injustice and work for equality. It's bad for business, and we have become very entrepreneurial and productive. In addition, we are just plain burned out — burned out answering the cell phones and our e-mail; burned out making those extra bucks to get the latest DVD player and the extra car. Justice for the poor will just have to wait. After all, it is their fault that they are poor (we say).

Do you feel the disappointment that I am feeling about the course of recent history? It is probably not unlike the disappointment many Christians experienced in the third, fourth, and fifth decades of the century just ended. The twentieth century began with such hope. It was to be the century when the world was to be Christianized — it was to be the Christian century. It was also to be a century that promised human progress, what with science and the Industrial Revolution creating all sorts of increased opportunities for prosperity. As we know, it did not happen. The World Wars put an end to the optimism. The Church may have grown in some parts of the world, but in Europe and America it has been losing ground for some time. Hopes have been dashed. Life is that way sometimes.

Almost two centuries ago African-Americans liberated from slavery were given all sorts of promises in the hopeful times of Reconstruction. But Jim Crow legislation and the ensuing evils of segregation broke those promises. Life is not fair, is it?

This Sunday's First Lesson portrays the sort of despair that comes when life's promises are broken. Biblical scholars are not sure about the historical circumstances of when our text was written. It is a complaint psalm very typical of a lot of ancient Hebraic literature.[1] Singing a song that reflected his despair about the injustices of life, the author of Habakkuk writes words that are timeless. The lyrics to his song capture the feelings you and I are likely to have when life deals us a tough time. Listen to his song now, because they could have been written for the injustice and lethargy of our times:

> *O Lord, how long shall I cry for help, and you will not listen? Or cry to you "Violence!" and you will not save? Why do you make me see wrong-doing and look at trouble? Destruction and violence are before me; strife and contention arise. So the law becomes slack and justice never prevails.* — 1:2-4a

The law has become slack and justice never seems to prevail. Standards are down, the law is slack, but if you have money for a good lawyer and a Capitol Hill lobbyist, you get what you want. "And justice [it seems] never prevails." In another verse, Habakkuk's song continues: "... judgment comes forth perverted" (1:4b).

Has he not told it like it is? The rich get richer, and the poor get poorer, and nobody seems to care. Habakkuk understands our times.

His song is about us. It is a song every one of us has sung when life gets tough, when it is not fair.

What do we do without disappointments and despair? Give up and retreat further into the private sphere, abandoning public agendas? A lot of so-called advocates of the '60s social justice and peace have done that. As one of the elders in my family has put it: "The [old] radicals are too busy on Wall Street today to care about the poor."

The author of Habakkuk did not let despair and lethargy prevail. He did not just sing that opening complaint psalm. He turned his despair to God: "I will stand at my watchpost and station myself on the rampart; I will keep watch to see what he will say to me, and what he will answer concerning my complaint" (2:1).

Oh, how we have a mouthful to say about God sometimes, especially when we have a complaint about life! "Where is God?" we ask when life does not go our way.

The author of Habakkuk had another song to sing, one that came from God. The Lord gave him, gave us, a vision (I would call it a dream), and it goes like this: "For there is still a vision for the appointed time; it speaks of the End, and does not lie. If it seems to tarry, wait for it; it will surely come, it will not delay" (2:3).

God's Word to Habakkuk, the Word of God for us in our despair, is a dream of the End. God points us to his final plans at the end of time, when the Lord's purposes for the world will be complete and when all the turmoils of life will make sense. "If that day seems to tarry," the Lord says, "wait for it." It will come. God is going to have his way with the world. All that fights against goodness and justice and happiness will not prevail in the final analysis.

God's way of giving us hope by pointing us to the End is typical of this Personal God of ours. When he sent us his Son, Jesus, the Son did the same. Think how often Jesus talks about the End Times and about the Kingdom of God. Mark, the writer of the oldest, and probably most historically authentic of the Gospels, was so taken by the emphasis Jesus placed on the End Times, that he summarized Jesus' whole ministry after his baptism this way: "Now after John was arrested, Jesus came to Galilee, proclaiming the good news of God, and saying, 'The time is fulfilled, and the Kingdom of God has come near; repent, and believe in the good news' " (Mark 1:14-15).

God always has been, is in Jesus, and will continue to be a God of the future. And that is a glorious word of hope! It is a glorious word, because when you have God's future, his kingdom in view, you have a perspective from which to critique the present. You are no longer chained by the heartaches, the dead ends, the insecurities, and the unjust structures of the present. You have an alternative. You have a new perspective on things and a hope that the way things are does not have to stay that way forever. And so the author of Habakkuk proclaims to us that even though the old dreams of justice and equality seem stillborn, even though we sometimes feel like we are on the treadmill with few alternatives, there is hope. New and better days are coming. God will see to it. Trust him.

The Black church in America has a long history of being sustained this way by a hope for the end times. (The technical term for this sort of hope for the end times is to call it an "eschatological hope.") Life may not be fair, but God is, and so the future has plenty of wonderful possibilities.

The slaves understood the Exodus story as a story about their future, about how God was going to set them free like the Hebrews were set free. And we all know about Martin Luther King, Jr.'s dream in his famous speech in Washington. In the midst of the injustices of segregation and all the turmoil of the time he proclaimed: "So I say to you, my friends, that even though we must face the difficulties of today and tomorrow, I still have a dream. It is a dream deeply rooted in the American dream...."[2] Can you and I dream that someday it will not matter if one is rich or poor, that one's children will get health care, that one day police racial profiling of minorities will end, that women will have the same per capita income as men?

Dr. King has other dreams. You know them:

> *I have a dream that one day on the red hills of Georgia, sons of former slaves and sons of former slaveowners will be able to sit down at the table of brotherhood ... I have a dream my four little children will live*

> *in a nation where they will not be judged by the color of their skin but by the content of their character. I have a dream today!*[3]

I have a dream that someday 11 a.m. will not be the most segregated hour of the week; that Black and white will live in the same neighborhoods and really get to know each other. The vision of the End and dreams of a just society go hand-in-hand.

Why has it not happened? Why is there still so much injustice, apathy, selfishness, and anxiety. Why is life still so unfair? The author of Habakkuk had that question. It is our question too. Listen to the song he sang to the Hebrews. He is singing it to us in response to all our hopelessness:

> *For there is still a vision for the appointed time; it speaks of the end, and does not lie. If it seems to tarry, wait for it; it will surely come, it will not delay. Look at the proud! Their spirit is not right in them, but the righteous live in their faith.* — 2:3-4

It has been 2,600 years since Habakkuk promised the end would not tarry. Jesus made that promise too. Were they wrong? Why are we still plagued with all of society's ills? Why is there still so much injustice, unhappiness, and lack of love among us?

Jesus, Habakkuk, and the Black church all say that the End is on its way. It is so close that you can catch glimpses of it! Martin Luther King, Jr., saw it the evening of his final speech. Here is how he put it:

> *Well, I don't know what will happen now. We've got some difficult days ahead. But it doesn't matter with me now. Because I've been to the mountaintop ... And I've seen the promised land. I may not get there with you. But I want you to know tonight, that we, as a people, will get to the promised land.*[4]

When you have caught a vision of what God has in mind for the world, when you know and truly believe in God's plan of justice and forgiving love, then you do not have to fear anymore. And when fear is vanquished, when you have confidence and trust in the future, that's when great things can begin to happen — because confident, trusting people are most likely to be society's change-agents. Such people are confident enough to act on their values.

How do we get that kind of confidence; how do we get to the mountaintop that Dr. King, Habakkuk, and Jesus talked about? I will tell you; these eminent Christians and our Lord can tell you; so can Martin Luther. If Jesus' words that the Kingdom of God has come near (Mark 1:15) are true, you and I have seen that Kingdom. Where? What does it look like? Martin Luther can tell you.

Writing in one of his most famous works for a general audience, Luther claimed that the Kingdom of God, that the End, is realized whenever we receive the Holy Spirit and that the Spirit is manifest in faith and in living godly lives.[5] Did you get Luther's point? The mountaintop, the vision of the End Times, is not hard to find. You catch a glimpse of it every time you believe, do good works, or see somebody else do a good deed. Of course for self-centered, selfish people like us to do those things it has to be a miracle! They are only possible because of the Work of the Holy Spirit. But such deeds do happen. Celebrate them; learn from them; praise God for them; take hope! More are on the way.

In the midst of all the chaos, despair, and hopelessness, there are plenty of indications that God has not given up on us and our society. Just as Habakkuk heard God proclaim that the End was coming to relieve the time of trouble, so you and I have that assurance too. Take heart. The troubles, the unfairness of life, will not last forever. God is going to take care of it. He is doing so this moment. The more faithful people he produces, the more sinners he justifies, the more good works will be done. And the more godly people and work he produces, the more heaven is realized here on earth, the closer he and we will be to putting an end to life's unfairness here and now. People who have been to the mountaintop, who have seen the End God has in mind, will be the real change-agents of the present.

Are you down in the dumps about life? Have you found yourself giving up on the dream of a just society? I ask you, then, two more questions: Have you believed what I am saying? Do you believe that you are justified by grace, have been made righteous by God (like Habakkuk and Paul say)? Then, behold, a miracle is happening in your life and in the lives of those around you! You have been to the top of the mountain, and glimpsed the End God has in mind!

Take hope. It will be that way for everyone someday. Come back down from that mountain, dive into life's problems, and you will make a difference! Believe the miracle, justified sinners. Habakkuk and God promise that things are going to get better, that you can contribute to it.

In the Black church they say: God may not come when you want him, but he's always on time. I say: Life's not always fair. God may not straighten things out just the way and when you want it done, but justified sinners know that he's already solved the problem. Behold those miracles of life, friends. See the good deeds those around you do, believe the gospel, and you'll see how God's straightened things out. Miracle of miracles: God might even use you and me in the end! What a miracle.

---

1. Childs, pp. 448-449, 451.

2. Martin Luther King, Jr., "I Have A Dream" (1963), in James H. Washington, ed., *A Testament of Hope: The Essential Writings of Martin Luther King, Jr.* (San Francisco: Harper & Row, 1986), p. 219.

3. *Ibid.*

4. Martin Luther King, Jr., "I See The Promised Land" (1968), in *A Testament of Hope*, p. 286.

5. Martin Luther, *The Small Catechism* (1529), III.8.

Proper 27 • *Pentecost 25* • *Ordinary Time 32*

Living Free

Haggai 1:15b—2:9

Why are things not better in America? With the booming economy, the new freedoms won by the Civil Rights movement and the Feminist movement, why is there still so much poverty, inequality, and discrimination? Questions such as these that we are asking today were on the lips and in the hearts of ancient Jews around 520 B.C. Many, if not most, of these Jews in Judah (southern Israel) at that time had been exiles in Babylon during the Babylonian Captivity. Some eighteen to twenty years before they had been permitted to return to their homeland after Cyrus the King of Persia had conquered the Babylonians.

There was initially great joy among the Jews. For nearly forty years they had been aliens in a foreign land. For decades before that time they had seen the power of their beloved nation wane. They had seen the great Temple of Solomon, the dwelling-place of their God, destroyed. But now they were home! The day of liberation had come; they were free. Could it be that the coming of God's Kingdom, the new era of the Messiah foretold by earlier prophets (like Jeremiah [31:27-34]), had been realized?

The problem was that during the period of Haggai's ministry, these hopes and dreams had been dashed. The returned Jews were living in impoverished conditions. The harvests had been poor due to droughts (Haggai 1:5-6, 9-11). They had not rebuilt the Jerusalem Temple, ostensibly they said because the time was not right (Haggai 1:4). But Haggai came to set them straight.[1] His words can set us straight today; by the grace of God, Haggai's insights can empower us to do something about America's social ills that we all lament.

Haggai's strategy in waking up his liberated (at least partially liberated) countrymen was to speak to the leaders of the Hebrews. People of God need to be bold in trying to bring about social, cultural, and religious change. Haggai was trying to move on all three of these fronts.

Religiously, Haggai's and God's agenda was obvious. They were committed to rebuilding the Temple which had been destroyed by the earlier Babylonian conquest. In essence, Haggai and God remind us that the key to personal renewal or the renewal of a nation rests with revitalizing and prioritizing the practice of faith above anything else.

Late in chapter 2, after our lesson for today ends, Haggai, on behalf of God, raises questions to the priests regarding proper worship practices (ritual cleanliness) (vv. 10-13). Apparently the people of Judah had not been observing all of the strictures on the performance of ritual sacrifices. Yes, Haggai's concern to put an end to the impurity had a religious motive, but it can also be interpreted as a call for cultural reform. In essence he was saying, "Let's get back to our heritage, to our cultural roots. Let's not let the oppression that we have endured in the past and our present dire circumstances lead us to forget who we are and the special things that make us unique as a people."

Finally Haggai addressed the question of economics. Yes, the people of Judah who had returned to their homeland were freer than they had been in Babylon, though not totally free. (The Persian Empire was still in control.) They had experienced some real hardships since returning home — poor harvests and even hunger (Haggai 1:5-6, 11). In such circumstances, can you blame them for not believing that they yet had the resources to undertake a big project like rebuilding the Temple (Haggai 1:9)? Would you have handled it differently? Was it just not responsible stewardship to take care of the physical needs like housing first?

Haggai and God seem to be saying that in order to break out of social stagnation you have to do bold things. If you do not, you merely continue doing business as usual, with all the oppressive features of your society still in place. Is this why American society still has many of its old disparities, despite some of the new freedoms won in the 1950s and '60s? Is it the case that we did not take enough economic and social risks in the waning decades of the century?

At any rate, Haggai's plan for curing the inertia of the people of Judah was to announce that God would find a way to bring the prosperity of other nations to Judah. (Perhaps Haggai embraced the free market and international investments.) The Lord says that he will bring such prosperity, because the gold and silver of the earth, all its wealth, belong to him (Haggai 2:6-9). God is in control, and he delivers his people.

In order for these economic initiatives to bear fruit, though, it would take work. And that is precisely the point of our First Lesson. It and the whole book of Haggai teach that this worldly political action, freedom, and divine intervention go together.[2] God sets us free, delivers his people, but we still have responsibilities to those set free with us. As the great American Reformed theologian of the mid-twentieth century, Richard Niebuhr, put it: "Responsibility affirms that God is acting in all actions upon you. So respond to all actions upon you as to respond to His action."[3]

Do you follow this point? Niebuhr contends that as you respond to the events of your daily life, act like you were responding to God's action. As you hear my words, respond as if it were God actually speaking to you. When you go to work tomorrow and a problem develops or the people you encounter are difficult, respond as if it were God with whom you are interacting. The person who is free does not *have* to do anything. But liberated Christians who believe that they are meeting God in their personal actions and in the socio-political dynamics of their day will *want* to get involved and serve their neighbors. That is how to "live free."

Martin Luther King, Jr., made similar points when he claimed that "freedom is responsibility." Failure to exercise this responsibility accounted in his view for why the new freedoms won for African-Americans had not solved all the social problems. As he put it: "The great majority of Americans ... are uneasy with injustice but unwilling yet to pay a significant price to eradicate it."[4] Most of the time we are not willing to live out our freedom responsibly.

Back in the sixteenth century Dr. King's insights were more or less endorsed by his namesake, Martin Luther. Of course Luther emphasized our freedom. The Christian, he claimed, is "lord of all, subject to none." But he also asserted that "a Christian is a perfectly dutiful servant of all, subject to all."[5] Living free (in Christ) involves service to God and our neighbors. Maybe the problem with American society today is that Christians have not been exercising their freedom in service, not really living free.

How can Haggai's stress on assuming socio-political responsibility be reconciled to an appreciation that God alone is our Savior and Deliverer, that all that is good comes from him? (I do not want you to hear this sermon as an exposition on what you and American Christianity *should* do to improve our nation's plight.) Once again Martin Luther offers some helpful insights. In a 1520 treatise when he talked about Christians as both lords of all and servants to all, he put it this way:

> *The inner man [the Christian], who by faith is created in the image of God is both joyful and happy because of Christ in whom so many benefits are conferred upon him; and therefore it is his one occupation to serve God joyfully and without thought of gain, in love that is not constrained.*[6]

The love that Christians show in exercising their freedom by serving others and by assuming socio-political responsibilities is not something that we *have* to do. God's grace has transformed you and me into people who *want* to take up these responsibilities. We do them happily and joyfully, Luther says. That is how you live freely. Freedom may entail a lot of work, but it is also a lot of fun.

Have we still given God the credit for all the good that happens through our exercise of freedom? In another passage Martin Luther compared the Christian to a cup into which God pours his love. God pours so much love into us that like a cup with too much in it that love flows out of us to our neighbors.[7] How are we still free? An empty cup does not have any cares and fears about spilling its contents. Christians, neither do you have to have any cares and fears about exercising your Christian responsibility. Doing that will happen as spontaneously as a beverage spills out of a cup that is overflowing. Of course God has enough love to fill up your cup and my cup, so that his love will spill out of us to others. That is freedom, the kind of freedom that makes us instruments which God uses to give his good things to his people.

We began this sermon by asking questions about why things are not better in America, why with the new civil rights freedoms of the '60s and '70s, there is still much poverty, inequality, and discrimination. It seems like the problem is that we Christians have not been exercising our freedom. Instead of exercising our sociopolitical responsibility or functioning as overflowing cups filled with all of God's goodness and love, too many of us have been in bondage to satisfying our egos and desires. Too often you and I have been mired in that kind of bondage. Like the people of Judah in Haggai's day, we have been too "busy" to care about spiritual things, too hung up on the latest trend to guard our traditions and values, too preoccupied with ourselves to address the political and economic ills of our nation. We have not been exercising our freedom; we have not been "living free."

The book of Haggai may give us an indication of something else that has gone wrong in American society. Some Old Testament scholars have noted that although Haggai sees a connection between the rebuilding of the Temple in Jerusalem and the Day of the Lord, there is no direct identification of this political undertaking (rebuilding the Temple) and the Kingdom of God.[8] Americans may not have been sufficiently sensitive to that insight. Too often you and I act like our favorite socio-political agenda is God's one-and-only way, *the* way of realizing his Kingdom here on earth, and that anyone who disagrees with us is not in touch with the truth like we are.

Haggai teaches us some humility. He and God teach us that we need to be open to our neighbors' exercising their freedom along with ours. Part of what is entailed in exercising your freedom is letting your neighbors be free by recognizing that even if they do not agree with your politics they may still be doing a Christian "thing." Think of the polarization in American society today. Is that polarization a little bit the result of demonizing our opponents, of not respecting their freedom, and of not conceding that they might just be doing God's "thing"?

Why is American society so flawed as we enter the new millennium? We have not lived as free as God has made us. Enjoy your freedom, friends; use it! Use it responsibly; use it to set others free. God is pouring his love into you, giving you all sorts of opportunities to serve him and to work to set others free of all that still binds them. God is pouring his love and all those good things into you. They are spilling out of you now. Let them flow. God's gifts are free for others, and so are you. Are you not glad that God has made us free? This nation and the world can be better because of your freedom and its responsible use. Live free, God and Haggai say!

---

1. von Rad, pp. 281-282.

2. For this insight I am indebted to Childs, p. 470.

3. H. Richard Niebuhr, *The Responsible Self* (New York: Evanston and London: Harper & Row, Publishers, 1963), p. 126.

4. King, *Where Do We Go From Here?*; Martin Luther King, Jr., "The Ethical Demands For Integration," *Religion and Labor* (May, 1963), pp. 3-4.

5. Luther, *The Freedom of a Christian*, in *Luther's Works*, Vol. 31, p. 344.

6. *Ibid.*, p. 359.

7. *Ibid.*, p. 371.

8. Childs, p. 470.

Proper 28 • *Pentecost 26* • *Ordinary Time 33*

A Vision
Of Freedom

Isaiah 65:17-25

Freedom is such a lovely word, a compelling image. What is freedom? How would you define it? What does it mean to you? Webster's *New World Dictionary* defines freedom as being exempt from control or from arbitrary restrictions. Freedom is said to be the ability to choose or determine one's own actions.

That was the sort of freedom, escape from foreign intrusion, which the Hebrews sought when our First Lesson was written. There is a lot of debate among Old Testament scholars about the circumstances of its composition. Most scholars agree that the book of Isaiah was written by at least two different authors, with only the book's first 39 chapters written by the historical Isaiah in the late eighth century B.C. The question is whether chapters 56 to the end of the book were written by a third author who is not the same as the Jew who wrote chapters 40 to 55 sometime after the end of the Babylonian Captivity.

Those who have concluded that there was a third author of Isaiah believe that he worked about the same time that Haggai did (sometime between 530 B.C. and 510 B.C.), sometime after the Jewish exiles in Babylon had returned to their Palestinian homeland. As we noted last week, this was an era of disappointment for the returning Jews. The golden age that they had anticipated was not happening (Haggai 1:5-6). Although free in the sense of no longer being under the rule of the menacing external control of the Babylonians, there was still a sense in which these Jews were not free. First, they were still under the thumb of a foreign power, Persia. Though these Persians were perhaps more permissive of their

Jewish subjects than the Babylonians had been, whenever you are subject to some external power, you are not free.[1] It does not matter if it is a good master or one who beats you. Either way you are still a slave. That was the Jewish condition.

Likewise, psychologists have observed that slavery leaves its mark on those enslaved. The experience of oppression keeps on oppressing, even after the external constraints are no longer in place. This was the situation that the Jews addressed by our text encountered. They were free. But in another sense they were really not free. The Persians ruled over them. Perhaps it was the scars of the Babylonian Captivity that still had them in bondage, had prevented them from restoring the Temple and fully exercising the freedom they thought they had. (After all they could not truly live out and celebrate their identity as Hebrews without that Temple and without restoring an heir of David as their ruler.) The Jewish exiles who had returned to Palestine may have thought that they were free. But in reality they were not.

How about you? Are you really as free as you think you are? "Of course I'm free," you say. "I'm an American." But how about those anxieties you feel or the regrets you have about the past? How about the old destructive bad habits which paralyze you? What of those desires, the egoism, that hold you in bondage? Are you really free?

Forget yourself for a moment, and consider the plight of your fellow human beings and of American society in general. Think of those trapped in poverty, addicted to drugs, victims of domestic violence, and war. Are they free?

We need to think about freedom in a new way. We need a new vision of freedom that will help us to appreciate how we are not free yet. We need this new vision to make us yearn for true freedom. And with that yearning, by the grace of God, we may be enabled to live in that freedom and be instruments of God to achieve it.

Our text today from the Old Testament has that vision. Let us hear its words again; the Lord God speaks through the text, and he says:

> *For I am about to create new heavens and a new earth; the former things shall not be remembered or come to mind. But be glad and rejoice forever in what I am creating; for I am about to create Jerusalem as a joy, and its people as a delight. I will rejoice in Jerusalem, and delight in my people; no more shall the sound of weeping be heard in it, or the cry of distress....*
> — 65:17-19

> *They shall not labor in vain, or bear children for calamity; for they shall be offspring blessed by the Lord — and their descendants as well. Before they call I will answer, while they are yet speaking I will hear. The wolf and the lamb shall feed together, the lion shall eat straw like the ox; but the serpent — its food shall be dust! They shall not hurt or destroy on all my holy mountain, says the Lord.*
> — 65:23-25

God will create a new heaven and a new earth, and we will rejoice. The wolf and the lamb shall lie down together, and there will be no more pain and violence. Isaiah's vision of freedom is not just a freedom for individuals. This is an inclusive vision, linking freedom to harmony, peace, and well being. Let's unpack this vision and see what it can mean for us today.

God says that he will create a new heaven and a new earth, and not remember former things. Of course we Christians believe that these words are prophecies about the coming of Christ and what he would accomplish. In Christ's death and resurrection, the ways of the world as we know it have been relegated to the past, and the future is open. All our sins, all our despair, all the scars of the oppressions of the past are gone. They belong to the former things that will no longer be remembered. When you get free of your old anxieties, your scars, and your self-seeking selfishness, it is like a fresh start, a new world. Are you hurting, anxious, or paralyzed by your past, by a destructive lifestyle, or by what society says you are? Our First Lesson points you to Jesus and proclaims that you have a fresh start. How's that for a new vision of freedom?

"Oh, but it is not quite so simple," you say. "I have known of Jesus and his resurrection my whole life, and I am still stuck in some of the same old destructive patterns." Is this text from Isaiah really relevant for you and me?

Martin Luther was lecturing on our First Lesson from Isaiah, and he dealt with the very questions with which we have been grappling. He wrote:

> *The Kingdom of Christ is not to be found there [while we live], but it rises to another place, where sense is not, but where faith is. So if I should feel sin, death, and evil and nothing good in my flesh, I must nevertheless believe in the Kingdom of Christ. For the Kingdom of Christ does not have its place in the senses.*[3]

Do not be surprised if you still experience your old imperfections. The new "you" whom God is making is on the way, and so is the new society where oppression and injustice are no more.

Strengthened by God's promise that brand new possibilities are on the horizon, that "the former things shall not be remembered," Christians like you and me can "be glad and rejoice forever" (Isaiah 65:17b-18a). As Martin Luther put it: "To the extent that one is a Christian he is joy."[4] Do you get that? The very essence of a Christian is filled with joy. How come so many of us, so many of our days, are sour, full of despair, aimlessness, and boredom? It is because we have not believed the words of our First Lesson. Believe them: Our Lord has promised to give you and me, this nation, this whole world, and all the universe a new start. We will be free from all the ugliness of the past that has bound us. Cling to that vision.

If you feel that your faith is too weak to believe this promise, the author of our lesson understands. The freed former Jewish exiles were asking those questions. Consequently in verse 24 of our lesson the prophet dreams of a day when, before we call, God will answer, and while we are speaking he will hear. Of course in Jesus Christ that day has already come. Again Martin Luther, when lecturing on our First Lesson, said it so well:

> *In the Presence of God our prayers are regarded in such a way that they are answered before we call. I wish that this promise were made use of to its utmost extent by all in all kinds of dangers ... In this state of despair we must cry to God, if not with our voice, then at least with our mouth. The prayer of the righteous man is answered before it is finished.*[5]

Before your prayer is finished, God has an answer. God has a plan for your life, regardless of how strong your faith is, regardless of the mess that you and I have made of our lives to this juncture. What a glorious, joyful vision. No wonder a Christian is joy (as Luther put it). When you have that kind of assurance, that kind of an affirmation of who you are, you are really free. Despair, guilt, dire circumstances can no longer have their way with you.

The message of the assigned First Lesson is also that this freedom is for everyone! After all, it says, God is not just answering your prayers and my prayers. He is not just giving you and me joy, forgetting all the mistakes of the past. He is creating a whole new heaven and a whole new earth to enjoy all these wonderful gifts and the freedom that goes with it.

When will that new heaven and new earth come? In a sense, as we have noted, it has come, or at least will soon come. It was initiated with the incarnation of Jesus Christ (Mark 1:14-15). But we can better discern how it has already come and what impact this vision can have on us today if we take one last look at our lesson, at its final verse (v.25).

We have noted how the text says that the wolf and the lamb shall eat together, that the serpent shall not destroy, that there will be no pain and destruction any more. When Martin Luther lectured on this very verse in 1529, he wrote words that apply directly to our situation. Here is how he put it:

> *Through his Gospel God can make the supreme tyrants of the world subject to a simple man and preacher, even though these tyrants were lions and wolves. God can turn enemies into friends. They shall feed together ... The kingdom of peace follows. They shall not hurt. The*

> *sum of everything: There must be a reign of peace among themselves. There will be peace without sword or force or tyranny, because there will be love, they will have the same inheritance, and everything will be the common possession of friends.*[6]

In this vision of the End, of the new heaven and the new earth, God turns enemies into friends. The institutions that have controlled us and American society as a whole will be subject to simple, ordinary people like you and me. There will be peace without forcing people to be at peace, because love will prevail. We will share the goods of the earth; wealth will be held in common. Do I hear the end of poverty and suffering prophesied? On that day all will be as free as you and I are, as free of anxiety as Christ has made you and me to be.

The Prophet is talking about "freedom" at this point, in its dictionary meaning. The peace to which he refers is freedom because there is no constraint, and recall (from the beginning of this sermon) that that is what the dictionary says that freedom is. This lesson proclaims, though, that real freedom is more than exemption from constraint. It includes community well-being; it includes harmony and peace; it includes love. The book of Isaiah (chapter 65) has given us a new vision of freedom.

When is that new freedom going to be realized? What does it have to do with us today? Can it help our nation? In the best traditions of the New Testament (because the first Christians expected the End to come soon and yearned for the New Jerusalem), the African-American church has believed that this new vision of freedom can make a difference how you live, even in the politics you hold. We all know of the dream that Martin Luther King, Jr., had at the famous march on Washington? But he had even more eloquent things to say about that dream and how it can change us and America. Hear him:

> *We shall overcome because the arc of a moral universe is long, but it bends toward justice....*
>
> *Thank God for ... [the] vision of a new Jerusalem descending out of heaven from God, who heard a voice*

> *saying, "Behold I make all things new — former things are passed away."*
>
> *God grant that we will be participants in this newness and this magnificent development. If we will but do it, we will bring about a new day of justice and brotherhood and peace. And that day the morning stars will sing together and the sons of God will shout for joy.*[8]

With this vision of hope and freedom, a freedom for all linked with a peace that makes old enemies fellowship together, with this vision of Isaiah and Dr. King we can transform America. That vision will not let you and me be so comfortable with economic disparity or with the ethnic and class tensions which mar this nation and this community. The writer of our First Lesson believed that this vision would transform people to whom he wrote. Can you feel that vision, that recognition that your freedom has to include freedom and security for everybody? In that case your life, your actions, and your politics will never be the same.

When will this new vision of freedom be realized? When will it happen? It has already happened in Jesus Christ. And if you believe this vision, if it starts transforming your life, then it has already begun to come about in you. The freedom that God gives is a glorious thing, because it sets everybody free!

---

1. Anderson, p. 154.

2. For these observations I am indebted to Karl Barth, *Church Dogmatics*, Vol. IV/1, pp. 311-312.

3. Martin Luther, *Lectures on Isaiah* (1529), in *Luther's Works*, Vol. 17, p. 388.

4. *Ibid.*, p. 389.

5. *Ibid.*, p. 392.

6. *Ibid.*, pp. 393-394.

7. Martin Luther King, Jr., "I Have a Dream," *Negro History Bulletin* 21 (May 1968), pp. 16-17.

8. Martin Luther King, Jr., "Remaining Awake Through a Great Revolution" (1968), in *A Testament of Hope*, pp. 277-278.

Christ The King Sunday

Salvation Includes Social Justice

Jeremiah 23:1-6

On this last Sunday of the Church Year (we call it Christ the King Sunday) our attention is directed to the reign of Christ — to his glorious reign which has already begun with the resurrection on Easter. It is a Sunday to think about salvation, because where Christ reigns salvation is effected. These themes are especially evident in our First Lesson.

Jeremiah conducted his ministry in Judah (the Southern Kingdom of the Hebrews ruled by David's heirs and centered in the great capital of Jerusalem) in troubled times. The nation had long been in decline. The Babylonian Empire had its sights on the kingdom.

Apparently the King of Judah and other leaders of the nation were functioning ineffectively in the eyes of Jeremiah (23:1-2). In response the Prophet predicted, in God's Name, that a new leader would be raised up. That new leader, "the Righteous Branch of David," would be the Messiah (23:5). We Christians then believe that we have in this text a prophesy or prediction of the Coming of Christ.

Jeremiah proceeds to proclaim what the Messiah would do, what salvation would be like. There are some surprises at this point. He does not refer to Christ's role in saving souls. No, it seems that in Jeremiah's view the Reign of Christ would have all sorts of political implications.

Although God's people are scattered, God promises to bring those who become exiles back home and to give them prosperity (v. 3). Fear will no longer be a way of life for these once-oppressed people. In fact, none of them will be lost (v. 4). Indeed, Jeremiah says, this Righteous Branch of David, the Messiah, "shall execute justice and righteousness in the land" (v. 5b).

When Christ reigns, the oppressed are restored. Justice is executed in the land. Do you believe it? Why has the Church so often overlooked this message? Could it be that we have been hung up on the wrong kind of spirituality?

The eminent American Christian social commentator, Reinhold Niebuhr, a man of significant influence on American politics from the 1930s through the '60s, noted this problem. In one of his later sermons he wrote: "Much of Christian teaching down the ages has been in terms of serving or saving the soul, but not the body. What we do in the body affects the attitudes of the soul."[1]

You cannot have a genuine Christian spirituality, you cannot have salvation, apart from the body. (Consider the Creed: We confess a "resurrection of the *body*," not an eternal soul.) And you are not concerned about the body if you are not also concerned about its welfare. Are the bodies around us receiving adequate sustenance? Are our resources distributed fairly to all, so that none are unfairly deprived? This brings us back to Jeremiah's claim that the Messiah will establish justice. Obviously, justice is the Christian's business. Ultimately it is God's business, Christ's business. After all, our Second Lesson (Colossians 1:15-16, 20) makes it clear that Christ created the physical world and redeems it, not just our souls.

How about the separation of church and state? From a Christian standpoint, the separation of church and state has nothing to do with *where* God rules (as if government were none of His business). It is about *how* God rules (using the Church to nurture our spirituality and the state to care for our physical-social well-being). How does God want the state to function? The answer is found in our First Lesson (v. 5). The ideal state over which the Messiah will preside will be one in which justice and righteousness prevail.

Perhaps you wonder about the relevance of this Messianic vision for our time and place. Well, Jeremiah was looking into the future, but Christ has come! The Messiah is among us. Christ already reigns. That is what we celebrate today on the last day of the Church Year! Consequently we Christians believe that these prophecies of the future, of the full revelation of the Kingdom of God, have been realized, or at least their fulfillment is on the horizon. Again Reinhold Niebuhr made an excellent point. He wrote: "The ultimate principles of the Kingdom of God are never irrelevant to any problem of justice, and they hover over every social situation as an ideal possibility...."[2] The Bible's vision of salvation includes justice.

What is justice? In the best traditions of both the Bible and Constitution, Niebuhr defines justice as the "balance of power."[3] This commitment entails that a preference should be shown for those with little power, notably for the poor. The poor deserve a preference in order to equalize their power with other socio-economic groups in society.

Certainly this idea that Christians are to give special attention to the plight of the poor and oppressed is all over the Bible, even if the Church has not always noticed it. "The Church's love for the poor ... is a part of her constant tradition."[4] This concern for the poor was embodied in Jesus' ministry (Luke 6:20-22; Mark 12:41-44; Matthew 19:21). Jesus' followers, both Paul and James, continued this concern for the poor (Romans 15:26; Galatians 2:10; James 2:1-6). Such a concern for the poor has all sorts of Old Testament precedent too, especially in the Prophets. Elsewhere in the book of Jeremiah this concern is explicit (22:16; 20:13). Isaiah (11:1-4; 14:29-32) and Amos (4:1-2; 8:4-7) proclaim God's concern about the poor.

An awareness that Christians like us have a special responsibility for the poor did not get completely forgotten after biblical times. There was a famous third century African bishop named Cyprian who told his priests: "Let your care also (as I have already often written) and your diligence not be wanting to the poor."[5] Fifteen centuries later the Church was still proclaiming that word. The new Catholic Catechism (based on the teachings of the Second Vatican Council) has put it this way profoundly: "Hence, those who are oppressed by poverty are the object of *a preferential love* on the part of the Church...."[6]

Do you get the point? Christians are always to show a preference for the poor. That means that caring for the poor is not just a matter of charity. Of course our congregation does that. We are often approached by people down on their luck, and we respond. But the idea of a preference for the poor means putting the poor's needs ahead of our building programs and salaries. It makes me think of what the great sixteenth-century reformer, the spiritual father of Presbyterianism, John Calvin once wrote:

> *Will not the Lord say, "Why have you allowed so many needy to die of hunger? Surely you had gold with which to minister sustenance. Why were so many prisoners carried off and not ransomed?..." To sum up ... "Whatever, then, the Church had was for the support of the needy." Likewise: "The bishop had nothing that did not belong to the poor."*[7]

Everything the Church has belongs to the poor. But if we are going to show a preference for the poor so that they can have power that means not just giving handouts, but working actively on their behalf in society as a whole. Wait. Am I suggesting a political agenda for the Church? Can you have salvation, can Christ be said to reign, unless there is justice, a justice for the poor?

In case you are still not sure about the answers to those questions, a prominent African-American Episcopal layman who teaches at Yale University Law School, Stephen Carter, can set you straight. He has noted the positive contributions that religious perspectives offer political life, how indispensable they are. Such perspectives, he says: "... provide approaches to the consideration of ultimate questions that a world yet steeped in materialistic ideologies desperately requires."[8]

Religious traditions like Christianity teach that means are as important as ends, that *how* you got there is as important as *where* you got.[9] In essence, this eminent Yale professor is saying, our faith teaches that it does not mean much if you have aquired wealth or fame by oppressing people with poverty. When Christ rules as King in your life, Jeremiah says, you will want to do all that you can to ensure that this nation's wealth is not at the expense of the poor.

That is not the way it is in the United States today. This is a society in which the gap between rich and poor is ever widening, even while the rich and many of us in the middle class get richer.

We are a nation that has turned to bashing the poor. We blame the poor for their own problems. It is their laziness, their lack of initiative, that has gotten them in the mess they are in, we say.

Few of us seem willing to concede that poverty might have to do with injustice, to an imbalance of power that rigs the system against the poor. After all, without money the poor cannot purchase much Congressional influence with campaign contributions. Because they live in neighborhoods where positive role models no longer want to live and inasmuch as they are without money to live near such role models, the next generation of the impoverished are less likely to break the cycle.

Why are we so blind to these dynamics? Why has our Church been all too silent? The words uttered by Martin Luther King, Jr., over thirty years ago, just before his death, could have been (should be) proclaimed today. Dr. King lamented: "And the tragedy is so often — these forty million [poor] people are invisible because America is so affluent, so rich; because our expressways carry us away from the ghetto, we don't see the poor."[10] We have effectively segregated ourselves from the poor. It is all about your sin and my sin. It is all about our selfishness.

Our celebration today of Christ the King Sunday reminds us that sin and selfishness, that all our efforts to forget the poor and marginalized, that our efforts to get wealthier even if it is at their expense and at the expense of justice, will not prevail. Christ reigns! Jeremiah in our First Lesson reminds us that under Christ's Lordship justice will prevail! No longer can the Church, no longer can our church, stay out of politics and remain silent about the plight of the poor.

When will justice be achieved and poverty ended? In a sense Jeremiah said that was in the future. In another sense with Christ that future has now come. Justice, the end of poverty, will not come tomorrow. But it is close. As Martin Luther King, Jr., put it:

> *There is nothing new about poverty. What is new, however, is that we now have the resources to get rid of it ... Today, therefore, the question on the agenda must read: Why should there be hunger and privation in any land,*

> *in any city, at any table, when man has the resources and the scientific know-how to provide all mankind with the basic necessities of life?*[11]

Do not give in to poverty, and the dream of justice remains alive. This is not a new command that Dr. King, Jeremiah, and I make of you. Overwhelmed as you and I are by the majestic love of God, awed by the Lordship of Christ, there is only one response that you and I can possibly make. Martin Luther believed that joy and love for our neighbors would inevitably flow out of us, like an overflowing cup. This will be a love that does not distinguish between friend and enemy, between rich and poor.[12] This is a love that will not forget Dr. King's question about why we still have poverty with all the bounty. When you know that you are saved, that God loves you, then you will yearn and work for justice in the land (Jeremiah 23:5) without any being lost and deprived (v. 4). That day has come; it is coming, my friends. Will you, will this church, be Christ's instrument by working for this justice? Amos 5:24 says that someday justice will "roll down like waters." Salvation always includes social justice, because the freedom of Christians includes everyone's freedom!

---

1. Reinhold Niebuhr, "Beware of Covetousness," in *Justice and Mercy*, ed. Ursula M. Niebuhr (Louisville: Westminster/John Knox Press, 1974), p. 68.

2. Reinhold Niebuhr, "Why the Christian Church is not Pacifist," in Larry Rasmussen, ed., *Reinhold Niebuhr: Theologian of Public Life* (Minneapolis: Fortress Press, 1991), p. 249.

3. *Ibid.*, p. 250; cf. James Madison, *Notes of Debates in the Federal Convention of 1787*, July 17.

4. *Catechism at the Catholic Church*, 2444

5. Cyprian of Carthage, *Letter To The Clergy* (c. 251), in Alexander Roberts and James Donaldson, ed., *Ante-Nicene Fathers*, Vol. V (2nd print.; Peabody, Massachusetts: Hendrickson Publishers, 1995), p. 315.

6. *Catechism of the Catholic Church*, 2448; cf. Vatican II, *Gaudium et Spes* (1965), p. 27.

7. John Calvin, *Institutes of the Christian Religion* (1559), IV.IV.8.

8. Carter, 273.

9. *Ibid.*

10. King, "Remaining Awake Through a Great Revolution," in *A Testament of Hope*, p. 273.

11. King, *Where Do We Go From Here?*

12. Luther, *The Freedom of a Christian*, in *Luther's Works*, Vol. 31, p. 367.

All Saints' Sunday

Why Earthly Powers Need No Longer Enslave

Daniel 7:1-3, 15-18

This is a story written for people who had been or were about to be persecuted, if not enslaved. (The book of Daniel was probably written in the mid-second century B.C. during a period of Seleucid [Syrian] domination in Palestine.) It tells them and us how their ancestors had once faced a similar slavery under the oppression of the Babylonians centuries earlier. The implication was that if these ancestors could endure and overcome such bondage, so could they and so can we.

Our lesson for this morning is the narrative of a vision or dream that Daniel had. Recall, Daniel is supposed to have been a Hebrew exile in Babylon sometime between 587 B.C. and 538 B.C. He was noted for his royal background, his good looks (Daniel 1:3-4), and the acclaim he received as a "psychic advisor" (interpreter of dreams) for kings (Daniel 2:19ff; 5:10-12).

The vision that is related in our lesson for today is the first of four that Daniel is reported to have had after his famous encounter in the lions' den and his subsequent vindication by the Babylonian Emperor Darius (Daniel 6:1-28). This dream and the others that followed are supposed to have transpired later when Belshazzar came to the throne (Daniel 7:1). Biblical scholars generally agree, though, that the real audience for this dream and the ones that followed were the Jews who lived in Palestine in the mid-second century B.C. when the Seleucid dynasty ruled and was engaging in religious persecution of the Jews. In other words, this may not be a dream of the historical Daniel, but one attributed to him by later Jewish writers.[1]

The whole question of who wrote this part of the book of Daniel and who actually had the dream really does not matter or undermine the Bible's truths and authority. You will see why it does not matter as we get into this dream. By reinterpreting a dream of Daniel for a new historical situation (one set in the period of the Babylonian Captivity into a time nearly three centuries later), the final editor of the book of Daniel has implicitly given us permission to apply this dream to our particular circumstances, more than two millennia after he edited the book.[2] This is a dream about the End Times. Let us see what it has to do with us.

Daniel dreamed about four beasts that came out of a sea — a lion with wings, a bear, a four-headed leopard with wings, and a dragon-like beast with horns (vv. 4-8). Each of these beasts seems to symbolize one of the empires which had plagued the Hebrews and held power over them at some time in the past. There is much speculation about what empires these beasts represent, but it is likely that the winged lion represents the Babylonian Empire, the bear the Medes, the four-headed winged leopard the Persians, and the dragon the Greeks (especially Alexander the Great) who were the most recent conquerors of Palestine and had established the Seleucid rule. Others believe that the four beasts symbolize the four kingdoms of the Emperor Alexander the Great whose conquest of Palestine had created the political situation of the Holy Land at the time the book of Daniel was composed.[3]

Of course it is just as significant to note that the intended references to the four beasts are never identified in the book of Daniel. This may be related to the fact that in Daniel, as in other Old Testament writings, the number "4" signifies completeness.[4] (The number "4" is evident elsewhere in Daniel, notably in chapter 2. In fact, the kingdoms of our First Lesson are probably the same as those of chapter 2, indicating that the text we now consider, though really a dream of the Daniel who lived centuries before the book was written, is in Daniel's heritage insofar as this new dream parallels and elaborates on the real Daniel's interpretation of a dream [in chapter 2]. That is why it does not matter who wrote our text for today, as the whole book is properly said to be in the heritage of

Daniel and so no distortion is made by the Bible by claiming that this dream is Daniel's. It is in his tradition.[5])

At any rate, the four beasts in our lesson also refer to completeness. We might say that they symbolize all the earthly powers. The story about this dream continues, and what happened next says something about our Bible lesson's relevance for you and me.

In verses 4-14 of Daniel 7 (not part of our assigned lesson) the last beast (the dragon with the ten horns) encounters "an Ancient One on the throne." Is it God? The dragon was put to death and the other beasts had their power taken away from them. Then the dream proceeds with a vision of "One like a human being coming with the clouds of heaven" (v. 13) who comes to God (the Ancient One), and the text reads: "To him [One like a human being] was given dominion and glory and kingship, that all peoples, nations, and languages should serve him" (v. 14a).

Who is this One like a human being? Some Jews have believed it to be a symbol for all faithful Jews. Others hold that it refers to the Archangel Michael. For us Christians, this is obviously a prophetic reference to Christ.[6] Our Second Lesson from Ephesians 1 (v. 22) makes this point.

The text continues in verse 15 which is part of our assigned lesson. Daniel is troubled by the dream. Consequently he asks for help in interpreting the dream's meaning. He gets it from one of the attendants to the Ancient One (v. 16). Is this one of the angels? Is that who interprets this dream? Or could we put a Christian interpretation on this text, one especially appropriate for today (All Saints' Sunday) and conclude that this attendant is one of the saints in heaven?

At any rate, this attendant interprets the dream more or less as we already have. The four great powers would have their day he said, but: "... the holy ones of the Most High shall receive the Kingdom and possess the Kingdom forever — forever and ever" (v. 18).

Who are these holy ones who receive the Kingdom? Does that refer to angels ruling the earth on God's behalf? Or is this text to be read as a witness (again so appropriate today for All Saints' Sunday) to the promise that in the End Times the saints (and that, of course, means all of us baptized in Christ) will rule?

Daniel, like the book of Revelation which is based on it, has long been a troubling book for the Church, not readily understood. Consequently the questions about who it is that will rule at the End are not so important for us at this point. The primary insight of this dream is that the earthly powers of Daniel's time will not ultimately prevail. Consider what that means for our nation and for you in your daily life.

A great African theologian of the early Church, Saint Augustine, claimed that power is what makes political institutions run.[7] Is he not correct? If the IRS had no power, would you pay your taxes? Without the threat of military or economic power, one government would never persuade another to cooperate.

Governments exercise power in illegitimate ways too. Consider the impact that slavery and later segregation have had on the African-American and Native American communities to this very day.

All institutions, not just those of government, operate by the dynamics of power (usually selfishly exercised power). Teachers have power over students (through the grading system). You go to work every day because if you did not the company could fire you or at least not pay you. We buy the clothes we do, wear our hair in the particular style we have, buy the goods we own, because the media exerts a significant power of influence over us. Indeed, increasingly the power of the media dictates the character of our family life and our values. Consider all the talk about the impact of rock music and video games on American youth, which were hot topics of discussion during the school shootings a few years ago.

In addition, social analysts are talking about how our economic system is also exerting power over us in the formation of values.[8] It is perhaps no accident that the emergence of feminism, with its discontent about stay-at-home motherhood, as well as declining loyalty to one's community and family ties are good for business insofar as these dynamics have swelled the workforce and created the flexible, mobile pool of workers which the new economy demands.

Can you see how much power the institutions of American society have over your life and mine? We are really quite powerless in some instances; we are merely pawns. There are some genuine similarities between us and the Jews in the years when the book of Daniel was written. We have both been manipulated for many decades by foreign powers.

Do you see how our First Lesson is Good News in light of our bondage to the power of our institutions? The whole point of the dream attributed to Daniel is that the power of social institutions is limited. Ultimately they will meet their demise. Only God's Kingdom is forever!

Daniel's dream is essentially a reality check for you and me, a Word of liberation. The earthly powers that exert so much impact on our lives need no longer have us in their clutches. The power of these institutions will ultimately wither away. It makes sense, does it not? Americans do not fear Russia as we once did, now that its power has ebbed. You and I do not fear our teachers since we graduated. One day, when comfortably retired, you will not be so concerned about the power of your boss or the company.

We know these truths already to some extent. But we continue to be in bondage to the same old institutions, to care too much about how Hollywood says we should behave or what the fashion industry says we should wear. Seventeenth-century French humanist and theologian Blaise Pascal described the ludicrous character of our plight so well. He wrote:

> *It is absurd to rely on the company of our fellows, as wretched and helpless as we are; they will not help us; we shall die alone. We must act then as if we were alone. If that were so, would we build superb houses, [wear the latest fashions, embrace the latest media values; conform to our company's culture], etc.? We should unhesitatingly look for the truth. And, if we refuse, it shows that we have a higher regard for men's esteem for pursuing the truth.*[9]

Is that not what we have succumbed to? We have made the esteem of our fellow human beings, especially the ones who exercise power in our institutions, more important than truth. Our text, the whole Bible, teaches that the truth is that our social institutions will not endure. By disregarding this we have set ourselves up for misery and unhappiness. According to Saint Augustine, you and I will only find happiness when we prioritize the values of God's Kingdom, the power of the gospel, over the values that earthly powers try to impose on us. Hear his words:

> *But the earthly city [and its institutions], which shall not be everlasting (for it will no longer be a city when it has been committed to the extreme penalty), has its good in this world, and rejoices in it with such joy as such things can afford ... These things, then, are good things and without doubt the gifts of God. But if they [human beings] neglect the better things of the heavenly city [the Gospel and its values] ... then it is necessary that misery follow and ever increase.*[10]

Now, when you realize that earthly powers will not endure, that it is the gospel and the things of God that have the real "staying power," then all those things that used to seem so important (wealth, power, reputation, your image in the community) do not matter as much. Relativizing earthly powers with the gospel sets you free from those powers, because the gospel puts you on the winning team. The gospel makes you a "lord of all, subject to none," as Martin Luther would say — one who receives the Kingdom and possesses it forever (Daniel 7:18).[11]

This sort of confidence that though earthly powers do their worst they will not ultimately prevail has been a great source of comfort to Christians over the centuries. It helped the early Christian martyrs endure. It empowered African-American slaves to "keep on keepin' on." Some say a view on life like this is too otherwordly and leads to passivity. But to realize with the book of Daniel that earthly power is relative, will not ultimately prevail, need not lead to political inertia. Let Martin Luther King, Jr., have a final word on that. In his final SCLC Presidential Address he wrote:

> *Now power properly understood is nothing but the ability to achieve purpose ... There is nothing wrong with power if power is used correctly ... Power at its best is love implementing the demands of justice, and justice*

at its best is power correcting everything that stands against love.[12]

Put the earthly powers in their proper place, Dr. King said. Be sure they are always subordinate to God and his love. Do not let the earthly powers ever do anything that contradicts justice, the Word of God, and God's love. When that happens, that loving God of ours will take our freedom and use it in the work of setting everyone free. Though earthly power tries to keep people down, we have a God who will prevail in the end and wants to lift up and crown (with freedom and justice) everyone who has been "sinking down."[13]

---

1. Westermann, p. 265; Childs, p. 615.

2. For these views I am indebted to the insights of Childs, p. 618.

3. Bruce Metzger and Roland E. Murphy, ed., *The New Oxford Annotated Bible* (New York: Oxford University Press, 1991), p. 1138OT; cf. Gerhard von Rad, *Old Testament Theology*, Vol. II, trans. D. M. G. Stalker (New York and Evanston: Harper & Row, Publishers, 1965), p. 311.

4. Shemaryahu Talmon, "Daniel," in Robert Alter and Frank Kermode, ed., *The Literary Guide to the Bible* (Cambridge: The Belknap Press, 1987), pp. 347-348.

5. This point has been made previously by Childs, pp. 618ff.

6. Metzger and Murphy, p. 1138OT.

7. Augustine, *City of God* (413-426), I.Pref.

8. For details on the power of the new economy, see Sennett.

9. Blaise Pascal, *Pensées*, trans. A. J. Krailsheimer (Harmondsworth, England: Penguin Books, 1966), pp. 80-81.

10. Augustine, *City of God*, XV.VI.4.

11. Luther, *The Freedom of a Christian*, in *Luther's Works,* Vol. 31, p. 344.

12. Martin Luther King, Jr., "New Sense of Direction," *Worldview* 15 (April 1972); 5ff.

13. For the images used in these concluding remarks, I am indebted to the rhetoric of one of the most prominent African Methodist Episcopal Church social activists of the first half of the last century, Reverdy C. Ransom, *The Spirit of Freedom and Justice* (Nashville: A.M.E. Sunday School Union, 1926), pp. 136-137.

Thanksgiving Day

God's Gifts Are Free: Enjoy!

Deuteronomy 26:1-11

Thanksgiving: How do we say thanks authentically and not lapse into the platitudes so often associated with this holiday? There are several dangers associated with the holiday. Ever since it was instituted as a national holiday by Abraham Lincoln, and even before when various state governors instituted it in their states, Thanksgiving has not been a strictly Christian holiday. There has been a lot of nationalism and self-congratulations associated with this day. What is the distinctively Christian way to give thanks to God for all the good things that we have? I want to start with the Old Testament because our Christian way of giving thanks is deeply rooted in Jewish precedents.

Our assigned Old Testament Lesson from Deuteronomy, though framed as part of one of Moses' long speeches to the people of Israel, is really a liturgy (an order of worship) of thanksgiving for the presentation of the first fruits of the harvest in the temple sanctuary. Included in this liturgy is a confession of faith.

What are these first fruits that Deuteronomy directs the people of God to give, and what does this directive have to do with us? We may have a church sanctuary, but that is not the same thing as the Hebrew temple. Besides, "first fruits" seem a little extreme. Ten percent maybe, but the very best? What about providing for our families?

Sixteenth-century reformer Martin Luther had a profound insight about these matters, and I want to borrow from his insights. Luther's point is that the "first fruits" refer to the very best things we have produced by our deeds: the good and beautiful things that we have made; the acts of kindness and love that we have done.[1] You might say, then, that the first fruits are works of Law, the righteousness that we think we have earned by keeping the Commandments of God. The first fruits are our very best deeds; they are the sort of things you do because you believe that God, society, and common decency require you to do them. We are proud of these good deeds. I am. Are you?

Luther makes a penetrating observation about all these good works that *we have done* and feel so good about. In one of his lectures on the book of Deuteronomy he wrote these words about such works of the Law:

> *For the Law first forces to works and when taken in the fleshly sense produces brilliant hypocrites, who imagine themselves to be the first of all, and to whom everything is due. This righteousness Christ killed by His passing-through (Hebrews 10:20), that is, his death, by which he taught that before God no flesh is justified by the works of the Law (Romans 3:20, 28) ... Therefore to offer up the firstborn and the firstlings is to confess that the righteousness of faith is accepted by his grace, not wrought by our powers.*[2]

Do you get the point? Thanksgiving is all about sacrificing your good works and good deeds before God. It involves recognizing that all your accomplishments are not your own. Give them up! Then you are truly prepared to give thanks for all that you have.

Something happens to you when you give up your good deeds in this way. When you stop trying to take credit for all the good things that you have done in your life, it becomes possible to give God the credit that he deserves for the good he gives through you. An awareness like that will not only make you thankful; God will use it to set you free. You see, the more you realize how God gives his gifts freely, without regard for your worthiness, the freer you will become.

Of course you and I cannot come to this awareness, achieve a spirit of thanksgiving, by our own powers. (When we try to make ourselves thankful, it is just more bondage, one more obligation hung around our necks.) I agree with Martin Luther at this point, when he says that we cannot really give thanks unless we are justified by grace through faith.[3]

When you have heard the gospel of justification by grace, then good works follow spontaneously. How can you not love one who loves you? God's saving love has a way of begetting good works. Faith becomes active in love, Paul says (Galatians 5:6). But the good works that this love produces that come from faith are not like the works most people do. I am talking about works of love that you do not *have* to do. These are works of which you take no ownership and in which you take no pride, because they are not your own. This is how you really say, "Thank You," to God and give him thanks.

We heard Martin Luther say this earlier. He claimed that the offering up of the first fruits to which our First Lesson from Deuteronomy refers (v. 2a) are the good things of love given to us by grace. The first fruits you give to God in thanksgiving are the service you and I render to God and our neighbors.[4]

You can understand now why Christians do not just give ten percent to God. Essentially when we are living the Christian life we are giving God everything. How about providing for myself and my family? If you ask that question, you have not gotten the point. Christians, every good thing that you and I have belongs to God. He has given them to you to use responsibly and to enjoy. But since they are not yours give them *all* back to God by thanking him for them and by sharing all these goods with those in need.

When you have this attitude, something wonderful happens to you and your outlook on life. Verse 11 of our First Lesson says that when offering their thanksgiving all the Hebrews, their priests (Levites), and even the aliens among them shall "celebrate." John Wesley, the founder of Methodism, interpreted this verse to imply that: "... it is the will of God that we should be cheerful ... in the enjoyment of the gifts of his providence."[5]

Be cheerful in enjoying God's gifts. Christians can be joyful and cheerful, because the good that they have is not their own. You and I are not defined by the good things we have in life. We did not even earn them. They are a sheer gift. That implies that if we do not have certain good things, do not have all the things we would like to have like wealth, beauty, power, or influence, that is not a negative reflection on you and me. All those things belong to God. No one *earns* them, and so you have not really failed if you do not have them. Can you feel the relief that insight provides? Can you feel the joy?

There is nothing that makes children happier than a gift. Well, children of God, that is what our Lord has done for you. He has showered you with undeserved gifts. People who realize how their lives are full of gifts will be happy. You will be so happy that you will not even need to try to be happy. That is what God has planned for you, and why he is so generous with his gifts. God wants us to be cheerful and happy.[6]

Appreciating that God is the One who owns all the goods we have in life makes us even more thankful people. The good job one has, the fine home, the wonderful family, you and I have not earned them. In fact we do not deserve them. We do not even deserve to see that beautiful sunset or to smell those roses. All goods are given to us (freely) on loan. Since we are not paying any interest on all these good gifts, we have a lot of reasons to be thankful. (You might not be as thankful if you thought that some of the good things in your life you had earned.) To know that all the goods you have in life are free gifts of God owned by him makes every day a Thanksgiving.

Appreciating that God is the One who owns all the goods we have in life can have one more wonderful outcome. It can set you free to enjoy those gifts even more.

Owning property is one of God's good gifts; make no mistake about that. But when there are problems with what you own, be it the car, the house, the expensive machine, it is an anxiety-producing experience (unless you are very handy with repair work). I know that when I encounter problems with the property I own, I sometimes wax fondly about the days when my wife and I rented. Then when a problem developed, it was not our problem alone to solve. Ultimately it was the owner's problem.[7]

Have you ever felt that way? When you are traveling, staying in that motel or hotel, it is a lot better when the roof leaks there than when it leaks back home, right? When it is somebody else's problem, life is a little simpler, and it is easier to enjoy things. When you are only borrowing something, there is a sense in which you are freer.

That is the way life is for you and me, friends. All the good things that we have belong to God, so "chill out" when problems seem to develop. Good caretakers of other people's property are careful with what is entrusted to them. That is what is involved in being a good steward of God's gifts. But ultimately the problems are God's, and he will take care of them. Is that not a liberating Word?

We surely do have a lot for which to be thankful, do we not? How much? Everything good that you have is on loan from God. You and I have not *earned* that great family, job, home, intelligence, and stature in the community by our hard work. Keep that in mind, and this will be a distinctively Christian celebration of Thanksgiving. You will not get caught up in nationalism and self-congratulations as is typical of America's version of the holiday as long as you keep in mind that all you have is a gift from God. The sixteenth century reformer, John Calvin, the spiritual father of Presbyterianism and the United Church of Christ, said it so well one time. Servants of God are strengthened by knowing that all is in God's hands, that all that is good is his. Calvin wrote: "Gratitude of mind for the favorable outcome of things, patience in adversity, and also incredible freedom from worry about the future all necessarily follow upon this knowledge."[8]

Knowing that all the good that we have is God's gives *incredible freedom from worry*. Incredible freedom. For if the good things that we have belong to God, even one's own life, then we can be confident that he will ensure a good and happy outcome of crises that concern his property. The good things that you have are not ultimately yours. Ultimately God will take care of them. Is that not a wonderful freedom? God's gifts really are free, friends. Enjoy! We can never get around to saying thank you enough for all these gifts.

1. Luther, *Lectures on Deuteronomy*, in *Luther's Works*, Vol. 9, p. 141.

2. *Ibid.*

3. *Ibid.*, p. 255.

4. *Ibid.*, pp. 141, 255.

5. John Wesley, *Commentary on the Bible* (1765-1766).

6. For this insight I am indebted to Martin Luther, *Table Talk* (1531), in *Weimar Ausgabe Tischreden*, Vol. 1, No. 124.

7. I am also indebted for this analogy to Martin Luther, *Commentary On the Sermon on the Mount* (1532), in *Luther's Works*, Vol. 21, p. 13.

8. John Calvin, I.XVII.7.

Lectionary Preaching After Pentecost

The following index will aid the user of this book in matching the correct Sunday with the appropriate text during Pentecost. All texts in this book are from the series for the First Reading, Revised Common Lectionary. (Note that the ELCA division of Lutheranism is now following the Revised Common Lectionary.) The Lutheran designations indicate days comparable to Sundays on which Revised Common Lectionary Propers or Ordinary Time designations are used.

(Fixed dates do not pertain to Lutheran Lectionary)

Fixed Date Lectionaries *Revised Common (including ELCA)* *and Roman Catholic*	Lutheran Lectionary *Lutheran*
The Day of Pentecost	The Day of Pentecost
The Holy Trinity	The Holy Trinity
May 29-June 4 — Proper 4, Ordinary Time 9	Pentecost 2
June 5-11 — Proper 5, Ordinary Time 10	Pentecost 3
June 12-18 — Proper 6, Ordinary Time 11	Pentecost 4
June 19-25 — Proper 7, Ordinary Time 12	Pentecost 5
June 26-July 2 — Proper 8, Ordinary Time 13	Pentecost 6
July 3-9 — Proper 9, Ordinary Time 14	Pentecost 7
July 10-16 — Proper 10, Ordinary Time 15	Pentecost 8
July 17-23 — Proper 11, Ordinary Time 16	Pentecost 9
July 24-30 — Proper 12, Ordinary Time 17	Pentecost 10
July 31-Aug. 6 — Proper 13, Ordinary Time 18	Pentecost 11
Aug. 7-13 — Proper 14, Ordinary Time 19	Pentecost 12
Aug. 14-20 — Proper 15, Ordinary Time 20	Pentecost 13
Aug. 21-27 — Proper 16, Ordinary Time 21	Pentecost 14
Aug. 28-Sept. 3 — Proper 17, Ordinary Time 22	Pentecost 15
Sept. 4-10 — Proper 18, Ordinary Time 23	Pentecost 16
Sept. 11-17 — Proper 19, Ordinary Time 24	Pentecost 17
Sept. 18-24 — Proper 20, Ordinary Time 25	Pentecost 18

Sept. 25-Oct. 1 — Proper 21, Ordinary Time 26	Pentecost 19
Oct. 2-8 — Proper 22, Ordinary Time 27	Pentecost 20
Oct. 9-15 — Proper 23, Ordinary Time 28	Pentecost 21
Oct. 16-22 — Proper 24, Ordinary Time 29	Pentecost 22
Oct. 23-29 — Proper 25, Ordinary Time 30	Pentecost 23
Oct. 30-Nov. 5 — Proper 26, Ordinary Time 31	Pentecost 24
Nov. 6-12 — Proper 27, Ordinary Time 32	Pentecost 25
Nov. 13-19 — Proper 28, Ordinary Time 33	Pentecost 26 Pentecost 27
Nov. 20-26 — Christ the King	Christ the King

Reformation Day (or last Sunday in October) is October 31 (Revised Common, Lutheran)

All Saints' Day (or first Sunday in November) is November 1 (Revised Common, Lutheran, Roman Catholic)

Books In This Cycle C Series

GOSPEL SET

Praying For A Whole New World
Sermons For Advent/Christmas/Epiphany
William G. Carter

Living Vertically
Sermons For Lent/Easter
John N. Brittain

Changing A Paradigm — Or Two
Sermons For Sundays After Pentecost (First Third)
Glenn E. Ludwig

Topsy-Turvy: Living In The Biblical World
Sermons For Sundays After Pentecost (Middle Third)
Thomas A. Renquist

Ten Hits, One Run, Nine Errors
Sermons For Sundays After Pentecost (Last Third)
John E. Berger

FIRST LESSON SET

The Presence In The Promise
Sermons For Advent/Christmas/Epiphany
Harry N. Huxhold

Deformed, Disfigured, And Despised
Sermons For Lent/Easter
Carlyle Fielding Stewart III

Two Kings And Three Prophets For Less Than A Quarter
Sermons For Sundays After Pentecost (First Third)
Robert Leslie Holmes

What If What They Say Is True?
Sermons For Sundays After Pentecost (Middle Third)
John W. Wurster

A Word That Sets Free
Sermons For Sundays After Pentecost (Last Third)
Mark Ellingsen

SECOND LESSON SET
You Have Mail From God!
Sermons For Advent/Christmas/Epiphany
Harold C. Warlick, Jr.

Hope For The Weary Heart
Sermons For Lent/Easter
Henry F. Woodruff

A Hope That Does Not Disappoint
Sermons For Sundays After Pentecost (First Third)
Billy D. Strayhorn

Big Lessons From Little-Known Letters
Sermons For Sundays After Pentecost (Middle Third)
Kirk W. Webster

Don't Forget This!
Robert R. Kopp
Sermons For Sundays After Pentecost (Last Third)

www.ingramcontent.com/pod-product-compliance
Lightning Source LLC
Chambersburg PA
CBHW071726040426
42446CB00011B/2242